HR DISRUPTED

It's time for something different

New and updated edition

LUCY ADAMS

First published in Great Britain by Practical Inspiration Publishing, 2021

ISBN   9781788602112   (print)
          9781788602105   (epub)
          9781788602099   (mobi)

Practical Inspiration
Publishing

Contents

Introduction to the second edition

The first edition of *HR Disrupted* was published five years ago. It was written to express my personal dissatisfaction with the way I felt HR was delivered by me during my career as an HR director, and countless other HR professionals. It was written as a call to action, to make HR more relevant for the disrupted world we all faced in the years after the Global Financial Crisis with its digital disruption, the relentless pace of change and the new expectations of work.

To be honest, I wasn't sure how it would fare. There are millions of books on changing business practices and thousands of HR textbooks. But it sold and continues to sell really well. More important to me, though, were the emails I received from HR professionals all over the world saying that they shared my frustrations and were excited about what I had written. That the book gave them hope and a renewed energy to make the changes they had long believed were necessary.

When my publisher suggested it was a good time for an update, I was initially very unenthusiastic. I really enjoy writing new material and ideas for our regular Disruptive HR blog and for our Disruptive HR Club (disruptivehr. club) members and am not particularly good at revising and editing stuff I've written in the past.

And then 2020 happened. And it seemed a good time to revisit the book.

Recently we have been hearing about things 'getting back to normal'. And whilst being able to travel, to not wear a mask in public and to hug my friends is really appealing, why in HR would we want to simply go back to normal? For all the sadness of the current crisis, it gives HR an amazing opportunity to do things better. To create a better normal. That's what this book tries to do. To create a better normal for HR.

Much of what was written five years ago still holds true; we are more disrupted than ever, HR still isn't keeping up, and there are definitely different and better ways to do it. But whilst HR remains pretty traditional, it is beginning to change, and I have seen some amazing HR innovations in the last five years. Moreover, the case for change has now gone from being a smart idea to a total no-brainer. So, the second edition has got new, more recent examples of how to do HR differently. But more importantly, it's about trying to reach out again, to shout even louder than the first time. It's time to do something different.

Part I

What's wrong with HR?

Human resources, HR, personnel – whatever you call the team looking after people in your organization, it's broken. This sounds extreme, but it's not a view I've come to lightly. My doubts about the way we HR professionals have been doing our jobs first arose around seven years ago while I was HR director at the BBC. In the five years that I have been running my company Disruptive HR, my conviction has strengthened. Then in 2020, of course, everything was turned upside-down. But the facts remain the same. HR is not fit for purpose.

This isn't to say I don't have a huge amount of sympathy for those who work in HR – it's not as if we have an easy life. We're being asked to deliver more for less, achieve greater productivity, and magic up more innovation. There doesn't seem to be a senior executive in existence who hasn't read about getting rid of appraisals and isn't asking what we're going to do about them; it seems to be getting harder, not easier, to make people work cross-functionally; and those pesky millennials won't stop demanding more flexibility. Then, just when we thought our HR budgets might increase for the first time in years, the financial director's begging bowl has reappeared. The problem is, despite the fact that all HR professionals face these same challenges regardless of their sector, the HR function isn't rising to them. So, what can we do about it?

In this book I'll be talking you through what's wrong with HR and how we need to turn conventional wisdom on its head. We must re-imagine our relationships with our employees, becoming slicker, faster, and more creative in our work with them. And to do this we must stop playing the company policeman and learn to be the 'people experts' in a radically new way.

I'll be talking to you as a fellow HR professional, although my thoughts are also relevant for anyone in a leadership position who sees people as the key to his or her company's success. Some of my ideas you may passionately agree with. Others you'll find surprising, even shocking, and a few you might downright dislike. That's all fine. I just want to provoke you into new ways of thinking about this amazing profession of HR, which I still love with all my heart.

I've also got some free resources which will help you tailor this book to your own needs, enabling you to see where you stand on these issues right now and to decide what changes to make for the future. Just head on over to http://disruptivehr.com/each-hr-diagnostic/ and take a look.

One thing's for sure: HR can't carry on in the same old way or it will be irrelevant before we know it. On the other hand, if we can transform the way we practise HR, we'll be turning our organizations into the winners of the 21st century. There's no time to lose, so let's get started with the reinvention of HR.

1

HR is dead (long live HR)

Almost any introduction to a book about business disruption risks sounding clichéd and tired, so let's just get into it. The business world we now live in is so different, so fast-moving, so disrupted, and so changed from the way it was, that the traditional methods of managing people are just not cutting it anymore. And I'm not just referring to the COVID crisis. They haven't been for some time.

This means everyone who's in the business of leading people has to find new ways of dealing with, or even creating, complex and rapid change. You need higher levels of creativity and productivity than ever before, which means the old style of relationship you have with your employees is no longer relevant. In your time in HR you'll certainly have experienced many changes in the way you work: saving money, driving up creativity, restructuring, and attracting new and different people are all on your agenda. But have you found ways to translate this into action? In my talks and workshops with HR managers and leaders I find this is the main challenge, and overcoming it starts with fully appreciating what it is you're dealing with in the first place.

So what does HR have on its plate today, and how is it different from before? I'm going to describe this by using my most recent experience as a proper HR director – at the BBC. While you may not have worked in broadcasting or the media you'll still be familiar with the BBC and the challenges it's facing. In addition, the BBC certainly isn't unique; it's a microcosm of the disrupted world in which all organizations live. Whatever business you're in, you'll have your own version of the ups and downs we faced.

There are seven main areas of change which HR needs to address. Let's understand what they are first, before we work out what to do about them.

1. Technology is transforming our businesses

I'm sure the way you watch television, listen to radio, and consume media generally has changed dramatically in recent years. When I was a kid, if I wanted to watch my favourite programme I had a choice between BBC1, BBC2, ITV, and then (oh, the excitement!) newcomer Channel 4, and I'd have to make sure I was sitting in front of the box at the allotted time in order to catch it. Fast-forward to today and all that has changed. My daughter recently came back from her around-the-world backpacking trip, and one of the first things she said to me (apart from 'Hello') was, 'Have I got Netflix in my bedroom? I want to binge-watch the second series of *Vampire Diaries* all weekend.' I had to restrain myself from telling her how lucky she was.

Today we 'time-shift' our viewing. Did you know 40% of drama programmes are now watched at a time when they weren't originally scheduled? When a new series comes out, my husband and I will install ourselves in front of it in one go – why wait an entire week for the next episode? Not only that, we 'dual-screen', which means tweeting or tapping on our laptops while we're watching the TV. Smartphones have brought a richer and more involved experience to the act of watching television, which has obvious implications for the way in which the BBC now has to produce its programmes.

What's more, the BBC doesn't have full control of its content any longer. Think of the reporting around the Arab Spring, much of which came from locals in Tehran and Egypt who filmed events with their smartphones and gained access to places the BBC couldn't go. That's a very different business model to the one in which the BBC would produce a programme for a scheduled time, and people would either watch it or they wouldn't.

So how does this relate to you? If you work in high-street retail, for instance, you'll be managing the impact of Internet shopping. If you're in banking, technology will have made massive differences to the way you work. If you own a restaurant, your customers will have checked out reviews of your place online before stepping through the door. It's easy to take for granted the changes technology has made to the way we do business, so it's worth pausing to consider what impact it's made on your sector.

From an HR perspective, technology's rapid emergence means we need our leaders not only to cope with fast-changing business models, but also to embrace and even create them. Have you got leaders in your organization who are thinking ahead about what's needed, and coming up with the ideas and methods to make it work? We've all seen what happens to those companies who haven't.

Often the best ideas for how to harness technology come from the younger generation, so HR needs to ensure these employees are managed in a way that inspires and excites them. Unfortunately, if your team is like most you'll be more concerned with driving costs down than ensuring you have an emerging group of staff who feel free to challenge the status quo. The old-style, command-and-control company structure is geared towards operational efficiency, not innovation and creativity.

2. Our competitors aren't who they used to be

Whenever I give a talk and ask those in the audience who have Netflix or Amazon Prime to raise their hands, a sea of arms instantly waves. What a change from the days when the BBC's main competition used to be good old ITV; it was so simple then, wasn't it?

But here's where it gets interesting. When I was at the BBC, broadcasters like Sky, Netflix, and Amazon Prime weren't just our competitors, they were also our collaborators and partners. For instance, when we realized we couldn't afford to bid for the Grand Prix broadcasting rights on our own, we teamed up with Sky. Similarly, the third series of *Ripper Street* was a co-production between us and Amazon Prime.

Your competitors aren't always the enemy anymore. They now come from places you don't expect, which means your relationships with them won't be as black-and-white as they used to be. We need to think about these relationships in a less simplistic way, which is a big shift for many senior managers. The problem is we don't generally have the skills and capabilities in our organizations to help them do that.

3. We're working in a collaborative, networked world

When I was at the BBC it was – like most organizations – essentially tribal. There was 'Tribe' News, 'Tribe' Television, 'Tribe' Radio, 'Tribe' Online, and so on. Getting these tribes to collaborate and co-operate with each other could feel like an insurmountable challenge. But today that's just not good enough; if an organization wants to adapt to change its employees need to be able to work together across functions and geographies. There are two reasons for this: to save costs and to provide a better customer experience.

A great example of cost saving is the way in which the Glastonbury Festival is now covered by TV companies. Until relatively recently, if you'd been at the event and wandered past the media area in your wellies, you'd have seen production crews from BBC Radio 1, BBC Radio 2, BBC 3, local news stations, and probably BBC News as well. But audiences don't really care which channel their Glastonbury footage is coming from – they just want to see the bands and hear the interviews. So now one in-house Glastonbury producer pulls together all the different teams, making it a more cost-effective and coherent experience for their audience; in fact, once the teams started collaborating, viewing and listening figures for Glastonbury rose 77% across all channels.

But the most significant way in which all businesses need to develop internal collaboration relates to my very first point: the Internet. In the 'old days' (which were actually less than 20 years ago), whenever the BBC created a new programme, such as *Strictly Come Dancing*, the production team would call the online department and say, 'Make us a website'. But audiences don't consume TV programmes and websites in isolation – they see them as separate parts of the same experience. This meant I had to find a way of getting the online and television departments working closely together, which was easier said than done. In the end it was only when fresh people led each department that we were able to create a properly joined-up experience for our audience.

If you're a retailer this is something you're already grappling with. In the past, when you stepped inside a department store, you would have had an experience very different from shopping on the company's website. That's all changed. Now you can buy an item online and pick it up in-store, just like you can with the major super-markets and many clothing retailers. As customers, this is something we're expecting companies to get right. But behind the scenes it's only created through collaboration between different leaders, and that's not happening as quickly as it should.

Think back to when you last tried to get disparate teams in your company to collaborate. It's tough, isn't it? And it's all down to the way in which we've typically led people; we've developed managers who focus only on their own budgets, staff, areas of expertise, and customers. Now we need to shift towards working from the customer backwards, ensuring our organizations can respond to the needs of the customer instead of those of the silo.

4. Organizations are changing structurally

Every HR person has grappled with organizational restructures, and it can feel like a thankless task. With many companies transporting work offshore, staff must be relocated to different regions or even countries. To have better relationships with our BBC regional audiences – who, after all, pay their licence fees no matter where they live – we moved children's and breakfast TV, sport, and Radio 5 Live from London to Salford, drama to Cardiff, and arts to Scotland. This was a massive shift for us and highlighted a degree of London snobbery in some of those who were expected to move. My favourite quote came from a senior manager: 'I can't possibly move north, I'm a vegetarian!' This is a small and rather silly example, but it shows the difficulties involved in managing geographic changes.

Managing virtual teams is the next challenge. I'm sure you no longer have everybody in your head office working 9–5 together; you're liaising across time zones, cultures, and locations. Many companies are still figuring out how to tackle the issues related to managing, developing, and leading people who aren't based in the same physical space and, of course, we are now facing the demise of the full-time office and a future hybrid of permanent home workers and occasional office contact.

5. Companies want more for less

HR managers are now having to make large-scale redundancies as a result of the current economic crisis. Of course, every business is under constant pressure to save money, Global Financial Crisis or not. But my point here isn't only about the cost-cutting; it's also about how it strikes at the heart of the traditional, paternal employee/ employer relationship. When pension schemes are curtailed, and terms and conditions are changed, it undermines employees' sense of entitlement that their organization is always there to look after them.

At the BBC we made 30% of senior managers redundant and closed our final salary pension scheme. The shock waves were not just financial but emotional: 'I assumed I'd have a job for life and you were going to take care of me and my pension.' What's more, in the public sector especially, many people feel their employers haven't replaced what they've taken away in security with the sweetener of a more modern and dynamic style of management.

6. The workforce is shape-shifting

This pressure to save money has also led to more zero-hours contracts and contingent workers, a situation which can be difficult to manage. For instance, everyone working in BBC Productions used to be on staff, but now for programmes like *Strictly Come Dancing* you'll find hundreds of people working for a brief period while the show is out, with the numbers plummeting to only three or four after it's aired. Television production companies have been operating with this model for some time now, but for many organizations this is a massive change.

Let's think about how it used to be. In most companies, an employee would join, go onto the payroll, and 'belong' to the organization. It was a solid, dependable, loyal relationship on both sides. But now this standing army of staff is only part of the story; when our workforce is largely made up of freelancers, as has been happening in the tech world for some time, we need to create a more agile training and talent management approach. How do we think beyond our standard boundaries so we attract the best people, but at the same time cope when our teams come together quickly and disperse?

The rise of the 'millennials', 'Gen Y', and now 'Gen Z', as they're sometimes called, is another challenge. Some people claim this group is completely different to how older managers were when they were starting out in their 20s and 30s, but I'm not of that school of thought. Whilst I don't think that you can ascribe a whole set of motivations and behaviours to a specific generation, I do believe the younger generations have a different set of expectations than their predecessors. They assume they'll have a level of autonomy, will be asked their views, and will have a voice at a relatively junior stage; they don't have the same sense of deference older people grew up with.

My heart sank when my daughter came home from college one day and said, 'I had to see the head of Upper-Sixth today.' Just as I was wondering what on earth she'd done to get into trouble, she explained she'd actually gone to complain about the standard of her

Chemistry tuition. I wasn't sure whether to feel relieved or shocked, but on thinking about it I realized it was just the millennial way. When young people are getting into debt to the tune of thousands of pounds for their degree, why wouldn't they be more demanding about their education? This feeds into their attitudes towards their employers. You may be of the view that we overindulge these kids, but then that's the way we've brought them up. We've asked their opinions from an early age so of course they want to have more autonomy, progress more quickly, and express their opinions more openly. And they're attracted to companies that show flexibility, agility, and a strong social ethos – in other words, a sense of purpose. They want their employers to have an ethical approach to climate change and to acknowledge and play a part in the fights for equality such as #MeToo and #BLM.

Multi-generational work teams are another new challenge. People now retire later than they used to, which can mean teams with up to five generations having to rub along together. Each has a different set of expectations about pay, contribution, and treatment. For example, older staff may want a traditional performance review whereas younger workers are more interested in what their peers think of them. How can we customize our management approach to these different ages?

Looking to the future, people now don't view retirement as that magical day when they turn into a full-time gardener. For many of us, retiring at 65 and spending 30 years without productive work is not great for our emotional and mental wellbeing. We might want to continue working but in a way that places fewer demands on us as we age. And yet most companies haven't caught up with this at all; we still assume the older someone gets, the higher up the career ladder she climbs, and the more responsibility she takes on.

7. The public are increasingly scrutinizing our leaders and finding them lacking

As I discovered only too well at the BBC, the final challenge to HR in this disrupted world relates to the increased public scrutiny all organizations are now subject to. This is closely linked to the rise of social media and also platforms such as WikiLeaks and Glassdoor (which, if you've not heard of it, is like a TripAdvisor for places to work, with millions of entries from employees rating their workplaces). The most insidious effect of this is the lack of trust we now have in our leaders. Let's see how the two are linked.

The Edelman Trust Barometer, a global survey run by PR company Edelman, analyzes who we trust in society. As you'd expect, as a result of the Global Financial Crisis our trust in leadership has plummeted, although this is recovering slowly. Almost every month we see once anonymous corporate leaders paraded across our television screens and social media newsfeeds, accused of various wrongdoings such as tax evasion; their motivations and personal affairs are also increasingly under question.

Individuals damaging corporate brands through activism is nothing new, but what's more recent is the destabilizing of *employment* brands. So exposés of companies which exploit their workforces are now an extra task for HR departments to handle, with the employees themselves often at the heart of the stings. Gone are the days when HR could send an internal memo to staff and it would remain within the walls of the organization (where are the walls now in any case?); if your communication isn't to someone's liking, it's on Facebook that evening on the way home from work.

This means lightning-quick responses are needed from both HR and PR teams, and yet the typical response from most organizations is simply to close down any debate as a control mechanism. Unbelievably, I still come across companies that ban the use of social media at work, seemingly oblivious to the smartphones in their employees' pockets.

So the growth of disillusionment in leadership coupled with the power of the individual employee to damage a company's reputation, at a time when we need trusted leaders more than ever in today's changing world, is creating a significant headache for HR. Leaders have to recognize that the old ways of communicating, managing the message, and being able to control it are long gone. And some are getting it. Spotify, for instance, encourages its employees to go onto Glassdoor and say whatever they like; it seems counterintuitive, but it fosters a huge amount of trust.

We're in a right royal HR mess, aren't we?

How do you feel now you've read this? Worried? Confused? Panicked? You're not alone. The main thing to focus on, though, is what you intend to do about it. And this is where it gets hard. Even though today's HR teams should be imagining a new relationship with their employees, in reality they spend most of their time talking about cost savings or restructuring. Does that sound familiar?

We in HR know this, but we're not changing our approach accordingly. We're still promoting the same kinds of people into leadership, we're still managing communications in similar ways, and we're still rewarding people the way it's been done for years. I've come to the conclusion it largely comes down to fear of change. Recently I worked as a consultant with an HR team on improving their processes, and they completely understood what they needed to alter. But when they focused on what they were actually going to *do* as a result, they felt very wary of trying anything different. It's a bit like wanting to lose weight; we understand we need to eat less and exercise more, but when we're faced with getting a personal trainer or trying a healthy recipe, we think of a million reasons why we can't do it.

Change is demanding and can be scary. Given the lack of positive role models in this space it feels like a leap of faith to do anything differently. Take performance management, for instance. Research shows 92% of companies have an annual appraisal scheme, but only 8% of them believe they're worth the time and effort that goes into them.[1] So why isn't HR doing anything about it? Because when we look at the potential alternatives we'd rather stick with what's been proven *not* to work than try something new that might transform things for the better. We think: 'Am I capable of change? Do I want it? How will this impact on my status? Will I fail?' These are understandable reactions, especially when there are plenty of 'experts' telling us the old way is best.

But we must be brave enough to acknowledge the need for greater creativity and productivity. Surveys continue to show that CEOs are not particularly happy with HR. And how engaged people are with their places of work on a global basis has remained static for the past 15 years. On all sorts of measures we're just not doing as well as we should be.

To remedy this we need our employees and leaders to do things in new ways – with different skills – and to use innovative technologies. We must ask them to create fresh business models, to work in different places – and with different people. This is a massive ask, and I'm going to help you with the 'how' later in the book. But first, I'll tell you a little more about me and how I came to this way of thinking.

Quick recap

- The business world was already changing rapidly and the crisis of 2020 has exacerbated that, so HR needs to change with it. The problem is that it's failing to do this successfully.

- Technology continues to transform the way we work, but HR is struggling to keep up.

- Changes in the way we view competition mean we need to reinvent the way we seek out counterparts outside our companies.

- Collaboration and agile teams are the norm, but HR is still too focused on the traditional organizational hierarchy.

- Demographic changes in the population are largely still not reflected in the way companies hire and promote.

- Companies can't hide their problems any more, but HR hasn't worked out a way of coping with this.

- HR must change or it will become irrelevant.

2

How I got here

I haven't always thought about HR this way. In fact, I've not always worked in this field. It was something I grew closer to once I realized how fascinated I was by the people side of change management. And because when I got my first HR management role I wasn't that experienced in this area, I listened to the experts on my new team. They told me the way to do remuneration was X and the way to do training was Y; I just assumed they knew best. You could say I swallowed the manual and regurgitated it.

Fast-forward a few years and I found myself, via an HR directorship at a large law firm and then a global corporate, appointed as the BBC's HR director. The environment was a major contrast to that of the blue-chip companies; journalists and media experts are always up for a challenge, and I soon learned they weren't keen on being told what to do. At first this was a headache, but it turned out to be the start of my turning point, as it was around this time a couple of incidents gave me doubts as to whether I was doing HR the right way.

The first was when I created a new performance management framework for the news department; it was absolutely textbook, representing what I saw as the highest level of thinking at the time around this subject. Excitedly I presented it to around 30 leaders in news, including

World at One, News at Six, and *News at Ten.* Those people were, and still are, among the most skilled and professional people in TV journalism. As I finished my presentation I glanced around the room, expecting a sea of nodding, appreciative faces; instead they seemed at best blank and at worst disgruntled. Somewhat disenchanted, I figured I'd not explained it well enough – surely they could see how this framework was going to help them deliver better news content and improve their productivity? But afterwards, one of the news managers who'd been at the BBC a long time said to me, 'Why are you always doing these things that are so demotivating for us?' I was shocked. I thought this was the last thing I'd been doing, and that I'd been giving him the tools and techniques to help him manage his team more effectively. It dawned on me then that what to me was a powerful framework was to him just another set of hoops to jump through.

The second was when we created a simplified pay and job competency framework for the BBC World Service. My team had slaved for months whittling down the layers from 18 to five – what a fantastic job we'd done, I thought. As I was explaining our thinking behind the new framework to the head of the service, I expected him to be delighted. But instead he sat patiently until the end and then said, 'I'm not sure this does anything for us except achieve HR neatness.' Again, I was stunned. I'd thought I was helping, but to him I was just stuffing people into boxes.

These comments resonated with me because they told me what I had already begun to suspect. Soon I found myself having doubts, serious doubts, about whether the traditional ways of working were having the positive impact on people I was told they should. I started to wonder, for instance, whether spending endless hours setting up an improved annual appraisal system was a better use of my time than questioning whether appraisals helped people to do their jobs more effectively in the first place. The problem was that I was so busy, regularly working 12-hour days; I'm sure you can relate to that. One Tuesday morning I looked at my diary and realized I had 14 meetings back to back (and none of them anything to do with changing the status quo). Each day, as I commuted in, I'd promise myself I would take some time to think about the bigger picture, but by the time I got back to my desk from meetings at 7.00 pm I didn't have the headspace for it. Instead I'd vow to do it the next day, and of course that day never came. Somehow it was more manageable to keep doing the stuff the HR textbooks told me I should be doing; at least no one could criticize me for that, could they?

Then came my personal and professional crisis at the BBC. It had started out so well; during the summer of 2012 the organization had delivered widely praised coverage of the London Olympics, trust and approval ratings were the highest since records began, and motivation levels amongst staff and managers were brilliant. However, it was not to last.

Six weeks later what became known as the 'Savile crisis' exploded; if you're in the UK you'll know what this was, but if not, it was the discovery that the now-deceased entertainer and BBC regular Jimmy Savile had been a predatory paedophile both inside and outside of the organization for many years. Handling the fallout from this was one of the toughest periods of my career, but my troubles weren't over after that. From then through to the following summer there were numerous other crises for me to manage, including strikes over pay and bullying allegations against certain members of staff. As HR director I became exhausted; it was a difficult time.

Just as I thought things might be calming down, the government's National Audit Office decided to review all the severance payoffs the BBC had agreed to over the previous three years. This resulted in my being summoned to give evidence at two Public Accounts Committees, a horrendous experience in which, amongst other things, I was accused of lying. The press then went to town on me. A national newspaper said I had 'killed off HR', dubbing me 'Lipgloss Lucy' because of my supposed obsession with designer labels and expensive handbags. My public image became one of a money-grabbing, unethical, and incompetent failure; this was reinforced by weeks of vitriol in the media, hateful tweets, and accusatory emails galore.

This finally led to my resignation from the BBC, after which I knew I would never find another HR directorship. Who would want to hire someone with as toxic a reputation as mine? But it turned out to be my saving grace, because if I'd gone to fill another corporate HR role not only would I have been miserable doing it the traditional way, but I also wouldn't have had the chance to *think*. I'd had doubts about HR for a while by then, and given that I was at that point the most notorious HR person in the UK (a phrase I never thought I'd write) I figured I would use them to start a much-needed HR revolution. My company, Disruptive HR, came into being. Born of my frustration with my beloved profession and my new mission to do things differently, it's an independent force in the HR world, aiming to transform the way we manage, lead, and develop our people.

First, I realized the starting point for the way HR traditionally sees things is this:

> *'We know best and we don't trust you as a manager or employee to do the right thing, so we're going to create*

*a process for you that you have to follow. We'll check
you've followed it (because we don't trust you), which
means we'll feel better because we know you're doing it.'*

Second, I began to see that all through my HR years
I'd been applying a clunky, one-size-fits-all approach to
workforces that were incredibly diverse. At the BBC, for
instance, a manager in his 50s who'd worked there all his
career was being treated the same as a young, second-job
Radio 1 producer; we weren't taking account of their differences in personality and career stage, or their preferences for how they wanted to be managed.

Finally, I discovered that although HR has been a
professional discipline for decades, it still has no real understanding of how human beings respond, build relationships, and are motivated. HR systems and manuals
are geared towards making HR feel better rather than
enabling employees to do their best work.

These were uncomfortable discoveries for me, to say
the least. But when I talk about these experiences with
HR managers in the workshops I give now, they laugh
and say, 'Oh – that's me too!' So I know I'm not alone,
and neither are you. I'm sure you've got a sneaking feeling you're not doing your job the way you'd like. When
was the last time you went to a dinner party and didn't
brace yourself for the inevitable eye-rolling when you
said, 'I work in HR'?

I don't want it to be like this, I really don't. Every HR
person I've ever met or worked with cares enormously
about what he or she does, works extremely hard, and
often takes a lot of flak. We all deserve better, but we have
to give better by providing the services that actually work
and make a difference.

There is a more effective way, and in the next section
I'll explain how HR should be.

Part II

The way HR should be: The EACH model

Fundamental change is needed to enable organizations to lead, manage, and train the people they need for the future in this disrupted world. But what should that change look like?

There are three elements to this, and they're encapsulated in the EACH model. What the model shows is this: in HR we must start treating our employees as **a**dults, **c**onsumers, and **h**uman beings.

In some ways it doesn't look that radical, does it? I imagine you reckon you already see your staff as autonomous grown-ups with the right to make their own choices and decisions. But by the end of Part II, I guarantee you'll be questioning pretty much everything you do and starting to look at your work in a completely different way.

If you're like most people, you'll probably find it tricky to judge where you currently stand on EACH without some outside assistance, so I've got a free diagnostic tool for you at https://disruptivehr.com/each-hr-diagnostic/. It will help you objectively see how you think about HR so you start off on the right foot. Why not give it a try?

Let's examine these three areas of EACH in turn. It's worth noting, though, that it's not about doing one, then the other, and then the next – this is a radical new way of seeing HR that depends on all areas of EACH hanging together.

3

Employees as adults

It had been a long day. Leaving my house in London at 5.00 am to chair a gruelling series of back-to-back meetings at our Salford offices had left me exhausted. Then, just as I'd been about to finish my day, I'd received a last-minute call from my boss asking me to prepare a report for the next morning. At long last I arrived at my hotel room. Slipping my key card in the slot and opening the door, I pictured myself indulging in a long soak followed by a flopping onto the bed with the TV remote. With a grateful sigh I kicked off my heels and opened the wardrobe door to hang up my jacket. And that's when I was confronted with one of the irritating situations of modern life.

I call it the coat-hanger effect. It's that feeling you get when you open your hotel wardrobe to find the hangers are the kind that stop you from stealing them, but are impossible to actually hang your clothes on. Don't you love them? Once, back in the mists of time, a few guests stole some coat hangers, and now every traveller is condemned to wrestle with the theft-proof replacements as a result.

So what does this have to do with treating employees as adults rather than children? It's this: when you consider the relationship HR managers have with their employees, 'trust' is not the first word that springs to mind. In fact, the starting point is more likely to be one of parent to child, and it generally takes two forms. Sometimes we see our staff as children who must be protected and can't be allowed to look after themselves, which leads to our taking a soft, almost indulgent approach. At other times we see all employees as potential rogues who could harm our organization, so we put processes and policies in place to protect the company at all costs (a bit like the coat-hangers above).

We're Mum and Dad

I realize I'm straying into the realm of gender stereotypes here, but please bear with me because it helps make things clear.

Let's look at Mum first of all. In some ways we can see the employer as Mum – caring and nurturing, she protects her charges from themselves on a daily basis. 'Mum Employer' thinks her people need lots of help at work, from pensions that are guaranteed to look after them in their old age to little treats like dress-down Fridays, and even to posters in the wash-room saying 'Now Wash Your Hands'.

What about Dad? How does he fit into this? 'Dad Employer' is the critical parent. Despite the fact that the vast majority of employees have no intention of damaging their organization, his starting point is that it must be protected against wrong-doers at all costs. This is manifested in things like multi-page employment contracts containing lists of policies that hardly anyone reads, HR procedures treating all staff as if they're potential troublemakers, and the end-of-term school report (or annual appraisal).

So much of what we do when we manage people at work, whether it be related to training, development, or management, is based on this old-fashioned parent–child relationship. I remember how one day, not long after I started at the BBC, it started to snow heavily. One of my team came to me and said, 'It's time to write the all-staff email.' When I asked what she meant, she said it was the one advising everyone to consider going home early because of the weather. I was amazed. Were we not able to trust our staff to look out of the window and make a sensible, adult decision about what they had to do to get home safely? Would they have waited for 'the email' if they'd been at a friend's house instead of at work? Of course not.

This wouldn't be so bad if we in HR carried out our parental duties consistently, but if we're trying to behave like parents, we're doing a pretty bad job of it. Financial pressures mean we're making people redundant, cutting their pay and pensions, and reducing their benefits. Families don't do that to each other, do they?

And irritating employees is only the start of it; there's a much deeper problem here. Not only is this parent–child relationship unsustainable in a modern age, but it also creates an environment in which people are unprepared to challenge authority, speak up, try something new, and take risks. How is the Holy Grail of greater productivity and creativity attainable when the company culture is one of 'wait to be told what to do, and if you don't do it you're in trouble'? Time and again I witness situations in which people are disempowered at work because they're treated like children. This has a knock-on effect, as employees become almost infantilized; they feel less ready to make responsible choices and expect their employer to make all the decisions around their welfare.

Challenge 1

*Next time you amend or create a procedure, ask yourself
if you're enacting a parent–child relationship without
realizing it.*

Complicated policies don't work in any case

My first major HR role was in the rail industry. Tragically, a sub-contractor died during repair works due to his not complying fully with the safety procedures – it was a terrible incident. Horrified by this, we did all the things you'd expect: instigated more training, increased the number of policies and rules around safety, put up posters, and re-vamped our communications. I then spoke to the staff on the ground, expecting them to be pleased with my efforts. Instead they told me that if they were to follow every rule in the book they'd never get anything done; they'd even become 'blind' to the rules. So the lowest-common-denominator thinking that assumes everyone needs to be protected, whether it be from deliberate sabotage, mistakes, or even from themselves, can actually have the opposite effect. The policies and procedures make HR feel better, but they're often at best ineffectual and at worst downright damaging for the employees concerned.

I saw this at the BBC as well. A producer had created a documentary about funeral parlours, and in doing so had filmed a dead person on a mortuary slab. He should have got the relatives' permission to put it on air but had not done so. Although thankfully the mistake came to light before the programme was transmitted, it was a terrible omission for him to make. In the meeting to discuss this, the editorial standards manager suggested training should be imposed to ensure people knew not to film dead bodies without permission. Really? To me, our real issue was that this particular producer didn't embrace the ethos of the BBC. We didn't need yet more rules and procedures. Instead of dealing robustly with this one individual we were about to patronize, annoy, and frustrate all our sensible employees who would never have dreamed of doing such a thing.

Challenge 2

Ask yourself whether your HR procedures are designed to protect your organization against any eventuality, rather than to help people do a better job. Because one thing is certain – there are not enough rules in the world to keep everyone completely safe.

More spoon-feeding equals less initiative

Our faithful Mum and Dad Employer often show a lack of trust in their managers' ability to lead their own teams. So many HR people I speak to are of the view that although their current procedures aren't great, they're necessary to ensure managers do their jobs properly. This results in the well-known annual round of compulsory appraisals, monitored and policed – of course – by HR.

My view is different. The best process in the world isn't going to make someone a competent manager, so shoe-horning him into a procedure to make him give feedback to his team isn't going to help. If someone is no good at managing then he shouldn't be in a leadership role in the first place.

I know what you're thinking. 'OK, I get it. I can see there's an unhealthy parent–child relationship going on here, and I've wondered about it myself for some time. But what about rules designed to protect a company against tribunal claims? My policies and procedures form a protection against us being sued.' This is a fair challenge, and one that's often posed to me. What I say to it is this: we live in a highly litigious world and I understand we need to cover our backs. I'm certainly not suggesting HR stops taking responsibility in this area, and in certain cases they need to step in and give clear guidance. But I think we can all agree the pendulum has swung too far.

In the Dutch town of Makkinga, for instance, local road officials felt the traditional plethora of road signs (70% of which were ignored in any case) treated drivers like children and discouraged them from thinking for themselves. So they removed the lot. The result? The number of accidents declined dramatically, as drivers started using their judgement more effectively. This 'adult-to-adult' philosophy is also behind Netflix's expenses policy.[1] Instead of creating reams of rules about what employees can claim for, their policy is five words long: 'Act in Netflix's best interest'. How refreshing to see a company treating its employees as responsible adults.

It even feeds through into training and development

Training is another area in which Mum Employer takes over. She puts on programmes aimed at increasing her employees' knowledge, but in fact we humans are incredibly resourceful when left to our own devices. If you're at home and want to find something out, do you book yourself on the nearest training course? Of course not. You Google it or ask a friend.

The way we train people doesn't encourage them to think for themselves or put what they've learned into practice in their jobs; instead, it fosters a classroom mentality in which time spent sitting at desks is seen as a valuable learning experience.

Challenge 3

Ask yourself whether the training you provide encourages your staff to think for themselves.

So far, so good. However, as you're reading this I'm sure you're muttering, 'Yes but...' a fair bit, and this is normal. I'll address a couple of the most common concerns I come across.

Yes, but... what if people abuse the trust we give them?

I'm often asked, 'What about the people who do something wrong? If we don't have rules around behaviour then how do we discipline them fairly?'

Of course we have to come down hard on people who act against the best interests of their organization. But remember, 99% of people aren't going to do anything seriously wrong. It's perfectly possible to create simple policies laying out the expectation that employees behave in accordance with the company's values and approach, without nailing every potential scenario down to the last letter. Of course this isn't easy, but it's so much more empowering and productive.

Yes, but... surely looking after our employees is a good thing?

This is a common feeling; in fact, I often hear employers refer to their staff as their family. But they're not family, are they? Because if they were, then HR would be the mum and dad and the staff would be the children. The reality is we're all adults together.

Sometimes people hark back to paternalistic employers like Joseph Rowntree as shining examples of employer philanthropy. It's true – in his day, when there was no social security and people worked in the same place all their lives, he was a visionary. But we live in a different era now, one in which employees want to make their own decisions (if only we'd let them). In fact, our whole HR model is based on the industrial age, which is why it's so ingrained within us.

It's possible to create an environment in which employees are treated as adults who will make mistakes but who will also be liberated by greater freedom. They can operate within a framework (I'm not an anarchist), but at the same time contribute more fully, and be more productive and creative, without needing to be micro-managed or told off if they get things wrong.

So what can we do differently?

There are three areas in which HR could remove this parent–child relationship, and by doing so liberate their staff to work more effectively in our disrupted world.

Start from a place of trust

Just imagine how different things would be if trust were the starting point for every policy and procedure you created. What would your expenses rules be like? How about your dress code? Would you need these control measures at all?

One manufacturing company changed its dress code from a multitude of rules to simply this: 'If you look in the mirror in the morning and have to ask yourself the question, "Can I get away with this?", then you should probably go and change.' It expects its employees to act like grown-ups who can take into account what they've got going on that day, and dress accordingly, just like they do in their personal lives.

A large insurance company has a simple approach to flexible working. Instead of a myriad of rules and policies, it says, 'Own the way you work', placing responsibility for finding the best way for its employees to be productive and achieve the right work-life balance with the employees themselves.

Google periodically asks its employees, 'What are the policies that frustrate you the most?' And when it gets the answers, it does something with them so everyone feels a little less frustrated and more willing to do an effective job. Maybe that's a good place for you to start. You might not be able to change or remove all your policies in one fell swoop (nor should you try), because some of them will be necessary. But you can certainly examine them and decide whether they could be lightened up.

Recently I spoke with a public-sector organization that asked its people which rules they found most restrictive. The main one was rigid working hours. So it extended the core hours from 5.00 am until 10.00 pm; employees could work within this time frame as long as they agreed between themselves how the office was covered. Not only that; it banished the traditional signing in and out procedure that made employees 'prove' they'd been there. The result was a huge uplift in morale and a retention of its best people.

When we trust our employees they're more likely to behave responsibly and be productive, creative, and forward-thinking. What would you change if your starting point was trust instead of control?

Encourage your staff to take responsibility for their own careers

When people go to work they tend to assume their careers are somehow their managers' responsibility. After all, it's the boss who sets up the performance review, gives them a grade, and sets their objectives.

I don't know about you, but when I want to achieve a goal (whether it be at work or home), I don't try my hardest with the tasks I've been told I *have* to do. And if someone's monitoring my progress and telling me off if I've not done enough, I'm even less motivated. Adobe, the creator of PDF software, has its own approach to this. It gives its employees the responsibility of seeking out conversations with their line managers about their performance in order to progress their career. Can you see the difference? If we could change how we manage performance from a hierarchical parent–child approach to a more equal relationship, it would encourage employees to think about how they could contribute. At the moment they're simply handing over responsibility for this to the HR police.

You may be wondering what would happen to the people who aren't proactive about their career and don't seek feedback. Well, if they show no interest in finding out how they can improve their situation and that of their employer, then would you want them in your organization? If you believe you've got to protect your company against people like that, all you end up doing is delivering a system based on the lowest common denominator. In my experience, and I'm sure in yours, the vast majority of people want to do a good job, are interested in their careers, and are keen to improve. But because of the way performance management is set up they simply wait to be told how to do it. This approach isn't delivering the kind of employees we need for the future.

Allow adult-to-adult communications

In this disrupted world, new technologies and alternative ways of working are increasingly the norm. This means HR often has to ask employees to do things differently from before, which can be scary for both parties. So whom do employees trust? Research increasingly tells us it's people like themselves – in other words, regular staff rather than senior management. And yet most corporate communications are top-down.

At the BBC we had an in-house magazine called *Ariel*. Faith in management was perennially low, but the magazine was always read cover to cover because it was editorially independent and written by 'everyone'. To be honest there were times when its critical views of management were uncomfortable, but I eventually came to see its value as a platform for all employees to communicate their thoughts with freedom.

How do we change?

Challenging the adult-to-child concept is hard because it questions the relationship that's grown up between employer and employee for centuries. When I talk about this in my workshops for HR professionals I'm often asked how we can start to change this culture, because if we've always treated our workforce like children, we can't suddenly let them 'play with knives', can we?

Of course, you can't instantaneously move from one extreme to the other, and I'll go into more detail on the best ways to implement change in Part IV. But I do think the problem lies less with the employees and more with their leaders. It's scary to cede control, especially when you've always been expected to know more than your staff. For now, let's just start thinking about how you can challenge your accepted ways of thinking while you go about your daily work.

Quick recap

- The relationship between HR and employees has traditionally been that of parent and child. This has led HR to play twin roles:
  - caring Mum, who doesn't like to let her charges think for themselves; and
  - disciplinary Dad, who creates policies and procedures based on the lowest common denominator.

- This approach is no longer sustainable in the disrupted world we now live in, because:
  - it's demotivating and frustrating for most employees; and
  - it discourages them from challenging the status quo and thinking for themselves.

- By treating people like adults we can increase productivity because they will feel more motivated, and more free to challenge the way things are done.

4

Employees as consumers

Picture the scene. It's Monday morning at a major high-street retailer and the weekend's sales figures are in. The marketing team files into the weekly meeting. First to present is the director of consumer insight, who showcases last week's findings on their customers' purchasing habits. She flips through graph after graph, detailing what they've learned about consumer attitudes, behaviours, and preferences, all of which helps them tailor their service to their customers' needs. Next is the head of loyalty data. He reveals that sales of high-margin products have increased now they're targeting their loyalty card offers more closely to buying patterns. Finally, to round things off, the marketing director announces that due to the company's regular research efforts and the clever customer segmentation they've implemented as a result, sales are up by a healthy percentage.

Have you ever had a meeting like this in HR? I'm guessing probably not. 'And why on earth would I have?', you ask. Let's look into that.

Something I've noticed over the years is employers lack the right terminology to describe their employees; if they're not referring to them as family (which, as we've seen, isn't appropriate), they're talking about them as assets. What an awful term. For a start, assets are objects like houses or cars – they're things you can predict will behave in a similar way to each other. One Fiat Uno is much the same as the next. But we all know people are messy, mercurial, and highly individualistic; they don't behave consistently and never will.

I appreciate employers usually mean the word 'asset' in a positive sense, in that they see their staff as being 'assets to the organization'. The problem with this word is that it's driven an approach to people which sees them as a homogeneous lump. In contrast, we can learn so much from consumer-facing organizations about treating people as individuals. These companies spend their lives obsessing over how to appeal to, retain, and change the behaviours of their customers. What if HR were to apply some of this consumer-based thinking to the way they develop their relationship with their employees?

If they did so, three radical and sequential transformations would take place.

- HR leaders would develop a deep level of insight into their people.
- This would encourage them to move away from a one-size-fits-all approach to employees.
- They would therefore design their procedures and processes around the users instead of themselves.

Getting to know – really know – your employees

As we've seen, consumer organizations have become unbelievably sophisticated in recent years. In your wallet you'll have a selection of loyalty cards, from your supermarket to your favourite department store or clothes shop. The grocery retailers are especially good at tracking your shopping patterns; they know that if you buy a particular toilet roll you might be tempted to choose a specific brand of yoghurt at the same time, so out goes a voucher to tempt you to add it to your basket. And it's not just the supermarkets that do this; banks have hundreds of models for deciding whether or not to give you a loan, and online retailers like Amazon have developed the cleverest algorithms on the planet. All consumer-facing companies treat understanding their customers, and acting on that knowledge, as a top priority.

In contrast, HR has two main data systems. The first is asset-based and, in your company, was most likely developed in the 1980s or 1990s (e.g., huge finance frameworks like SAP or Oracle with their bolt-on human resource management tools). In terms of insights about your employees, they tell you what you've got, how many, how much they cost, and possibly your staff absenteeism levels and projected retirement dates. They're great as drivers to save costs, but they tell you nothing about how your people think, feel, make decisions, or might behave in the future.

At my gym, however, there's a touch screen near the exit which asks me how my visit was that day. When I check in with EasyJet, they want to know what I thought of their service. Each time I leave a hotel I'm asked for feedback (maybe I should mention the coat-hangers). Tesco has a consumer research programme in which its representatives go into people's homes every three to six months for hours at a time, in order to get to know their customers in a deep way.

And what do we have in HR? The annual engagement survey. You know the routine in your company – suddenly it's survey time. First there's the big fight about the questions to ask, with some departments wanting to focus on certain topics in a specific way, or to increase or reduce the number of questions they're allowed to include. After many weeks you finally agree on your 25, 30, or 80 questions, depending on how successfully you've negotiated with the various leaders involved. The next battle is when you're going to hold it. Department A is about to make redundancies so it's a bad time for them; Department B has a big project going on so their staff won't have time to fill it in. Despite this, at long last you agree on a date.

Then you encourage (or rather, hassle) all your employees to fill it in, and get a 60–70% completion rate. Once the scores are back, they're aggregated to such a high level to ensure confidentiality they're meaningless to most managers. And the result? Surprise, surprise, most people want higher-quality training, more pay, better communications, and improved career development. Weeks of action planning by managers then follow, along with communications from HR to make sure employees know about all the great things they're doing for them. At which point it's time to start the whole process again.

Does this sound familiar? Fortunes are spent on these annual engagement surveys and yet global statistics show employee engagement has remained static for the past 15 years. Something isn't working, and HR doesn't understand what it is because we don't know a lot about the people who are supposedly our most important asset.

Challenge 1

Ask yourself honestly how much you know about what your employees think and feel, and what evidence you have for that.

How can you get to know your employees?

HR data systems are never going to become like Amazon overnight – there isn't the time or money for that. But there's still a lot you can do.

Check in with your staff more frequently

Doing a grand survey once a year isn't enough, but doing a complete survey of all staff more often isn't practical either. Some companies, however, do regular pulse surveys with small sample sizes using the plethora of online tools that are now available to us. Belron, the windscreen replacement company, sends a weekly text message to a sample of its employees asking the question, 'How was work for you this week?' The company can then respond to issues immediately as they arise.

Identify the data you need to predict the future

Wouldn't you love to know how your staff might behave if you were to change your grading structure, amend your appraisal system, or alter your recruitment policy? There is a way, and it entails picking one important issue and asking how you can find the relevant data for it. This takes time and effort so you can't do it for everything and everybody – just pick one area at a time. For example, a US bank wanted to understand how it could retain more of its good people. It tracked its staff over the course of three years and found the key factor in predicting whether or not an employee would stay was sideways movement in the organization which broadened their skills. Someone with a linear trajectory who'd successfully gone for promotion after promotion was more likely to leave. Furthermore, when it compared its findings with line managers' personal predictions, it realized how much more accurate the hard data was. What did it do once it discovered this predictor? Given that broadening their skills was the factor most likely to encourage employees to stay, it gave its most talented people lots of opportunities to do this within the company. And it worked.

Travel more deeply into your staff's minds

This is the old-fashioned one. Although line managers don't always know everything about their team members, they can usually tell you what training and communications from HR they prefer. Qualitative research is the backbone of most consumer organizations' consumer insight tools, after all. When was the last time you chatted to managers with the aim of finding out what their people really think? The Co-op supermarket holds regular sessions called The Colleague Voice designed to really understand how its people feel about the way they are managed and developed. The regular conversations give it fantastic insights into what it should focus on, what it should change and, most importantly, how it should deliver to them.

Segment, segment, segment

People always look at me weirdly when I talk about segmenting employees into groups, because segmentation isn't a standard expression in HR. But bear with me on this, because it makes a huge amount of sense.

In HR we typically design processes to meet two needs:

- **compliance:** forcing managers to do what we don't trust them to do on their own (even though the better leaders do it regardless); and
- **our own convenience:** making processes scalable so everybody can take part regardless of experience, monitorable so HR knows when they've been carried out, and one-size-fits-all so they're cheaper and easier to implement.

The problem with this approach is it doesn't take into account the needs of different types of employees. When people feel their preferences are ignored, their response is either to dismiss the requirement or to comply with it as grudgingly as they can get away with.

The classic example is the annual procedure that 92% of organizations participate in: the appraisal. Although some appraisal systems differentiate between leaders and team members, rarely do they offer more than minimal personalization. All employees are shoehorned into one process so HR can tick a box and claim they're managing performance. I'll be going into what's wrong with appraisals in more detail in Chapter 9, but for now let's just recognize them as entirely unpersonalized.

Successful consumer organizations don't start with themselves; they start with their market. They find out every detail they can about the customers they're aiming at; this shapes their branding, route to market, pricing, and advertising, so they can tailor what they do to different groups. Rarely do we take this approach in HR, but Virgin Trains is an honourable exception. It asked its market research department how they would go about assessing and segmenting their 3,500 employees. Instead of taking the asset-based approach, which would have meant asking questions such as 'How many?', 'Where are they?', 'How old are they?', and 'What are they costing us?', it looked at aspects such as social media preferences, traditional media consumption, learning biases, and so on. It called this internal market research the Amazing Colleague Experience, and it went far deeper than any employee engagement survey. All of the rich data was then used to inform the creation of meaningful, employee-driven initiatives.

Challenge 2

*How would you instinctively group your employees –
by age and length of service, or by more meaningful
measures? It's easy to fall into the trap of assuming
'how many' is more important than what they think
and feel.*

Design your processes around your users, not yourselves

Going back to consumer organizations, user-centred design is central to how they operate. The product or service development process isn't complete until customers have had their say on it. When Chrysler, for instance, was launching what became dubbed the 'dashboard of the future', it buddied its trial customers with local engineers and product designers and as a result identified an almost universal need for a bigger dial on the stereo. Given that the development of this new dashboard was critical for Chrysler's credibility as a brand, this was an important finding.

And yet HR continually develops new processes without involving the very people who'll be at the receiving end of them. When I arrived at the BBC I was amazed to find many of my team who were responsible for writing policies for people in TV or radio had never actually visited a production on-site, been to see the news go out, or watched a radio broadcast being put together. Naturally I challenged each team member to find a production to visit so we could end this ivory tower approach. One of my staff went to visit the set of *Luther*, a production on which people worked long hours outdoors with minimal office facilities. She couldn't believe that only the previous month she'd designed a process in which all new temporary workers had to copy their passport and email it to HR within 24 hours. How were real people on the ground ever going to comply with that?

So what can you do differently?

Treat your employees as ready-made focus groups just waiting to be asked their opinion. The accountancy firm Grant Thornton knew it needed a new travel policy, but it didn't want to impose it unless it was realistic for everyone to comply with. With that in mind, it put it on its intranet and asked for employees' views. The feedback from office-based staff was positive, but it was deemed impractical for those on the road. Rather than feeling disheartened, the HR team changed it over the weekend to something more employee-friendly.

You can go further than just using your employees as research – you can involve them in the development of an entire process. Adobe wanted to redesign its recruitment experience from the perspective of potential new employees. It broke the process down into how its brand was represented, how easy it was to use, and what impressions the applicants gained of the company every step of the way. The starting point was what it wanted its users to experience.

Quick recap

- Seeing employees as assets dehumanizes them – instead, see them as individual people with their own preferences.

- Treating employees as consumers leads to three major benefits:
  - deep insights into your people;
  - movement away from a one-size-fits-all approach; and
  - procedures and processes designed around employees rather than HR.

- Understanding your staff requires more effective research methods.

- Meeting the needs of your people means testing your processes and policies.

5

Employees as human beings

I sighed. It was no good putting it off – I had to accept it was time for me to send another all-staff email. As you can imagine, my communications at the BBC rarely contained good news; they usually announced pension changes, pay freezes, or some other choice item from our cost-cutting programme. Sadly, this email would be no different. I looked it over one last time. Had it been approved by the internal comms team? Check. Had the press office given it the once-over? Check. How about the employment law team? Again, check. Was there a word out of place, or a phrase that could come back to bite me? No, it all seemed okay. As I pressed 'Send', I felt a heaviness in the pit of my stomach and braced myself for the barrage of abuse that was sure to follow.

No sooner had it gone out than my phone rang. It was Jim, one of the guys in the newsroom. 'Can I give you some feedback on your emails?' he said.

'I guess so.'

'They're crap. You should really get someone else to write them for you.'

'Okaaaay...'

'Seriously, they're terrible. Because they're just not *you*.'

Deciding to take this as a compliment, I scrolled through the last few all-staff emails I'd sent. 'He's absolutely right', I thought. I'd been so keen to get my emails watertight I'd stripped them of all humility and humour, leaving them pompous and sterile. I'd adopted the royal 'we' and, in an effort to be accurate, had 'lawyered out' any trace of my individual personality. No wonder they were badly received; who wants bad news from someone who doesn't even seem to care?

Jargon and acronyms

Unlike the previous two chapters, which focused on treating employees as adults and consumers, and could be directed at leaders as much as HR professionals, this one is much more about how HR has made a rod for its own back. Like any profession, we've developed our own language. We love our acronyms and jargon, don't we? As a result, we've made ourselves look a bit mysterious and opaque, which has led many managers to feel nervous around us in case they get something wrong. Maybe they're concerned about inadvertently breaking the law, or they might be worried about discrimination. And the highly structured processes and formulaic approaches we've created because we don't trust managers to do the right thing don't help.

We need to put the human back into human resources, and there are two elements to this:

- developing a deeper understanding about how employees function as human beings; and
- thinking about how we can create more human leaders.

Challenge 1

Run your next communication through a 'jargon filter' (or even better, ask someone outside of HR to do it). Or check out this list of HR phrases to avoid https://disruptivehr.com/nobullshithr/.

Understanding your employees as human beings

Whenever we in HR face a challenge, we typically create a process in response. If we need to ensure our talent is moving around the organization, for instance, we'll develop a talent management process. If we want to put succession plans in place, we'll produce a succession-planning grid. And if we want to improve productivity and performance, we have the annual appraisal process. We've created these systems partly to make life easier for ourselves and partly because we don't trust managers to do the right thing without them.

The problem is, these procedures don't work for *people*. Humans aren't easily boxed up into categories. So what does work? Fascinatingly, in the last 20 years, with the introduction of MRI scans, psychologists have been able to discover so much more about how our brains respond to different stimuli. This is opening up a whole new world of insights into human motivation and behaviour. There are many models which are helpful for understanding this, and I'm going to share three of my favourites with you.

The SCARF model

Created by neuroscientist Dr David Rock, the SCARF model shows how our brains respond to threats and rewards.[1] In his view, we instinctively react to these in ways similar to other animals. There are five main threats.

- **Status.** According to Rock, our brain treats the threat of loss of status in almost the same way as physical pain. In many organizations, for instance, managers increase their sense of status by enhancing their job title to include the words 'senior' or 'executive'; any attempts to streamline these titles will meet with fierce resistance. It's a powerful, instinctive reaction.
- **Certainty.** We like to feel safe, but as we know in this disrupted world, volatility is the norm. For instance, people usually feel more anxious about the threat of redundancy than the news it's actually happening.
- **Autonomy.** We want to be able to do our job in our own way. Alternatively, this could relate to threats in our physical environment, such as changing to an open-plan office; I remember an engineering colleague once 'building' his own office in the corner out of archive boxes (he naturally made it like Fort Knox).
- **Relatedness.** We instinctively prefer to work with people we know and trust. When we're asked to work for a new boss or collaborate across teams, we can feel threatened.
- **Fairness.** This is the one that makes the least sense from an animal perspective, and is a uniquely human response. When we see one of our colleagues being treated unfairly it has a dramatic effect on us. This negative response to unfairness can often rear its head in redundancy or bullying situations.

When any of these threats arise, the part of our brain which handles fight, flight, or freeze gets flooded with blood and we 'shut down'. In real terms this means we get angry, sulk, or become paralyzed or overly emotional. I'm sure you've seen all these reactions when you've introduced changes at work. However, the converse is also true. If we're rewarded with elements of the SCARF model, with *increases* in status, certainty, autonomy, relatedness, and fairness, the part of our brain which controls learning, creativity, problem-solving, and lateral thinking is opened up. We're freed to work more effectively.

Think about how much more work in HR is centred on creating threats rather than rewards. We focus on policies, thereby preventing people from having an increased level of autonomy; the parent–child dynamic creates a feeling of reduced status; and any kind of management change encapsulates a whole range of these threats. If HR understood more about how human brains function and applied that knowledge, we would do many things radically differently.

Challenge 2

Take a look at today's to-do list and calculate the percentage of your work centred on threats as opposed to rewards.

Dan Pink's motivation model

So we've seen what doesn't motivate people, but what does? Dan Pink's[2] excellent research-based book *Drive* explains how people are intrinsically motivated and questions whether money is actually the big driver we think it is. For his book he carried out a range of experiments which reveal that the huge amount of time we spend trying to work out how to motivate and reward people through money is largely wasted. In fact it can often do the opposite.

According to Pink, there are three things which motivate us.

- **Autonomy.** The more control we have over our lives, work, and physical environment, the more incentive we have to perform better. This is similar to Dr David Rock's view of autonomy.
- **Mastery.** We love to become better at things we're already good at. This builds our self-esteem and means we can concentrate on doing what we enjoy.
- **Meaning.** This relates to having a purpose – a connection to something bigger than ourselves.

And yet when we look at how HR approaches these three areas, we can see it's lacking. I've already talked about autonomy, so let's move onto mastery. Typically HR trains people on a remedial basis. If someone is great at commercial activity but less good at interpersonal skills, she will be sent on a course to make her better at influencing people. But other research shows if you're not very good at something, chances are you're never going to be anything better than mediocre at it. So why is the entire training industry based on getting people to be well rounded (in other words, slightly better at something they're not very good at), rather than on encouraging them to be excellent at what they already do well?

When I first arrived at my HR role at Eversheds, the legal firm, I asked my boss, 'What makes a great lawyer?' He said, 'There are three types of lawyers: finders, minders, and grinders. A finder is great at winning work – an extrovert and good at sales. A minder is a fantastic team leader who gets satisfaction from helping trainees grow and develop. A grinder is a technical expert who loves delving further and further into his or her specialism – the grinder isn't good at sales but lives for the intricacies of the law.' I thought this was interesting enough, but then he said, 'You rarely get lawyers who have more than one of these traits, and it's almost impossible to find someone who's good at all three.' And yet that's what we do in HR: try to get people to be good at all three.

Thinking about Pink's discovery regarding how important meaning is to human motivation, let's ask ourselves how we can help employees to connect to something bigger. At the BBC our purpose was to inform, educate, and entertain; this was a real motivator for those people who got it right, and was far more powerful than a few extra quid on bonus day. And yet in HR we don't spend anywhere near enough time thinking about how we can ensure our people feel they're part of a larger and more meaningful whole.

Left brain/right brain

This is the third psychological model. The idea that our left brain is centred on logic and analysis and our right brain on stories and creativity won't be new to you. All of us clearly have both parts, although some people are more left- or right-brain-focused than others. But my main point is if people are to be fully engaged they need to have *both* sides of their brain activated. So what does this mean for how we communicate with and train people? Especially, what difference does it make for leaders when they're wanting to understand how people respond to their messages and intentions?

Most communication from leaders is left-brain-oriented. Think of the typical presentation crammed with data and analysis – all facts rather than stories and emotions, which we humans respond more strongly to. I'll explain more about how leaders can motivate through understanding human psychology in a moment.

Ironically, we 'get' all this psychological theory instinctively in our private lives, and yet as soon as we set foot in the office we apply a different set of rules. If you've got children, for instance, you'll know they're not easily motivated by logic alone; if one is sporty and the other academic you'll have a natural feel for how to encourage them in ways that are right for them. Equipping people for the unfamiliar and disrupted world at work may be less about HR's training people to do new things and more about applying what we already know about human behaviour.

Helping your leaders to be human

Life is tough for leaders; in this increasingly volatile and disrupted world, they need to have enormous capabilities. But what does HR really do for them? First of all, we promote people into positions of leadership because they're the best at what they do. So the most competent accountant gets the finance director role; the most skilled journalist gets promoted to editor. But as we've seen from Pink's work on mastery, promoting people away from their core talent and expertise is not the way to go. We *don't* need leaders to be the best in their field, but we *do* need them to be able to get their team members to deliver the very best work of their lives. Nor can leaders have all the answers, because nowadays nobody does. Instead of appreciating this we promote the people who are high-ego, charismatic, and good at a command-and-control way of working; they're not necessarily the people who can get the best out of others.

Second, at the same time as expecting more and more from leaders, HR dilutes their humanity by expecting them to use 'leadership language' and conform to certain behaviours. I've seen some managers carry out job interviews in which they don't even make eye contact with the candidates because they're so busy filling in the HR checklist for the perfect recruit.

It's just as bad when leaders give presentations. Before I did my first session with the senior leadership team at the BBC, I was a bit nervous. The director general had said to me, 'Now Lucy, when you do this speech you need to know most of your audience are ex-journalists. They like facts, data, and evidence – none of your wish-washy HR stuff.' So I did a fact-based, analytical presentation just as I'd been told. And it bombed; they pulled my data apart and were clearly not engaged with what I'd been trying to say. When I asked myself why, I realized my talk had failed because I hadn't treated them as human beings.

What is it with leaders who feel the need for a 35-page PowerPoint with graphs of EBITDA and all sorts of other statistics when they talk to their people? Don't they know what people really want? People are desperate for a human being up there who can help them understand what the facts mean to them personally in a story. They also want to know what their leaders themselves *feel* about their subject, and to see humility and humanity in their communications. This all takes confidence for leaders to do – it's not easy to show our inner selves, especially in front of an audience.

I'm sure you're familiar with the O.J. Simpson trial. It's a fantastic demonstration of the power of the story over hard facts. The prosecution in this case had all the data on their side: the DNA, the sightings, the blood traces, and so on. It should have been a slam-dunk case for them. But the defence took a different tack. Essentially they said, 'Let me tell you a story. A story about police corruption at the LAPD, about black versus white, and about power versus innocence.' They won a case that had originally looked unwinnable, not through facts but through telling a more powerful and meaningful story.

Helping leaders be more human in their communications is where HR should be coming in. We're trying to create trust and a higher level of engagement between them and their teams, and we're not going to do that with a sterile, corporate communication style. What are we doing to give our leaders the confidence to be themselves?

Challenge 3

Next time you create a PowerPoint presentation, have a go at stripping out most of the numbers. Does it make you feel uncomfortable?

Having said that, we are where we are, and we've got the leaders we've got. So what can we do about this? Here's where it's fascinating to look at the work of top-five executive-search firm Egon Zehnder.[3] It researched what leadership capabilities we need for the future and came up with five key attributes.

- **Resilience.** The quality that allows people to be confident and resourceful in an uncertain world.
- **Engagement.** The ability to motivate people to be the very best they can be.
- **Curiosity.** The motivation to find new ways of doing things. We know sticking to the same old patterns and approaches isn't necessarily going to serve us well in the future, so being alert to fresh ideas will allow our leaders to thrive.
- **Insight.** The knack for spotting connections between people or ideas. If you think back to

Chapter 1 and the need we have now to anticipate new business models, a leader's ability to create a vision wider than his or her own business area is vital.

- **Humility.** My favourite. This is one of the key character traits that encourages people to trust their leader.

To me, this is an excellent overview of the very human qualities we'll need from our leaders in the future. We also need to help our leaders have the confidence to be more human. We can do this by:

- getting them to recognize what they're already good at and see how they can use these talents to develop their own style of leadership;
- celebrating the human approach when we see it;
- encouraging them to make it personal, by bringing in examples from their lives outside of work; and
- not stripping out the human elements of their communications.

So what can you do differently?

Look at your processes and ask yourself if they show any understanding of how human beings actually behave. I'm especially thinking of your performance management system; is it creating many of the threats Dr David Rock identified? Many organizations trying to bring the human back into human resources are now calling appraisals 'conversations' instead of 'performance reviews'. Hearst Publishing, for instance, decided it was going to have career conversations, and it totally changed the dynamic. Suddenly the appraisals became adult-to-adult and were therefore unthreatening, as the uncertainty was taken out of the process.

You can also look at your reward and benefit structure and ask yourself if you're relying too heavily on cash bonuses to incentivize your employees. Compass, the industrial caterer, asked its staff what benefits they would most value, and now tailors benefits to the job types; chefs, for instance, who are on their feet all day, get a healthcare package which addresses postural problems. Many businesses are also moving away from individual, and often divisive, bonuses towards team or group rewards. How about giving your employees a menu of benefits to choose from, such as extra holiday or extra pay? This allows for alignment with their own values.

It's not easy, is it?

If you're like most people I speak with, you're feeling some resistance to this way of thinking. And I sympathize, because I've only managed to get this far after two or three years of developing these ideas. We all have deep-seated views of the employer–employee relationship which can be very difficult to shift. But what I say is this: sure, this new way of thinking doesn't feel safe or familiar, but what's the alternative? Carry on as you are? Because if you do, HR will slowly lose its relevance, credibility, and fitness for purpose.

Quick recap

- HR has become increasingly de-humanized through its language, the processes it develops, and the lack of support it gives to leaders.

- Processes treat people as things, not humans.

- Several helpful psychological models show how human minds work; from these we can learn how to motivate and reward people more effectively.

- Leaders must develop the confidence to be better and more authentic versions of themselves.

Part III

Reinventing HR

You've learned what's wrong with HR today and you've discovered how it should be through my EACH model (treating employees as adults, consumers and human beings). If you've not taken advantage of my free diagnostic tool I encourage you to give it a try at this point, as it will help you discover where your thinking (and that of your organization) stands right now. It's at http://disruptivehr.com/each-hr-diagnostic/.

Now you're going to find out what you need to do to reinvent HR in your workplace. I'll take you through each of the main functions of HR in turn, so you can see how to transform your department into one that's fit for the 21st century. If you find yourself wondering just *how* you're going to do all this, don't worry. In Part IV I'll be giving you lots of help with the best ways to implement change. For now, just see this as a guide to what needs to happen.

6

Recruitment

When my phone rang at home I didn't expect it to be my friend Emma – we hadn't seen each other for at least five years. 'How are you?!' I exclaimed, surprised and delighted she'd taken the time to get in touch. I love a good catch-up with an old colleague.

'I'm fine, everything's fantastic', she said. 'I'm getting married in a couple of months and I'm applying for a new job. It's all go.'

We started to update each other on our news, but after a few minutes I began to sense something wasn't quite right. 'Are you okay?' I asked.

'Oh yes, great. But I was just wondering', she said, 'this job I'm going for – I know the other main person in the running and she's really good. I think you know the guy who's interviewing me, so I was wanting to ask – and don't worry if you don't want to – but would you be able to put in a good word for me?'

And that's when I realized. Lovely though it was to hear from Emma, the reason she'd called was because she wanted something from me. Of course I was happy to help as I knew she'd be great for this role, but I couldn't help feeling disappointed as I put the phone down. She'd turned our friendship, with all its positive emotions, into the kind of transactional relationship where we only make an effort when we want something in return.

And that's what we in HR do when we advertise for jobs, isn't it? We have a vacancy, we advertise it, we interview the applicants, and then we offer one of them the role. Rarely do we bother to think about our potential employees before we need them, and anyway, what's the point? Actually, there are plenty of reasons to think ahead before we need someone new, but first I'll analyze how we currently attract candidates to our organizations. Then I'll talk about how we decide who gets the job.

What's wrong with traditional candidate attraction methods?

I used to say this to my managers: if you're filling a position for which the salary is £50,000, plus 20% for pension and National Insurance and the cost for induction or onboarding, that takes your first year's investment to around £70,000. Throw in the advertising or recruitment agency fee and you've spent £80,000. That's a lot of money. And yet when we recruit in a transactional way we make a hiring decision incredibly quickly without building up any kind of relationship with the applicant beforehand. It's a system that lends itself to error. Whereas if you already have some knowledge of your potential candidates, you're able to understand who they are, what drives them, and what excites them, which makes your decision a much more informed one.

Another disadvantage of the transactional, linear method of recruiting relates back to my experience with my friend Emma. If you only go out to the market when you need someone, it doesn't encourage your candidates to feel terribly warm towards you, does it? On the other hand, if potential employees are already aware of your company as being a fantastic place to work, they're more likely to want to put their best efforts into your recruitment process. This also attracts the best employees to you – flexible, enthusiastic, committed people.

I have to hand it to HR and say this is an area where we've upped our game recently, especially in agile and innovative industries such as digital technology, in which the war for talent didn't abate during the Global Financial Crisis. In fact, the changes are linked to the digital trend itself – social media, online video, and of course crowd-sourcing sites like Glassdoor. The availability of these platforms means no matter what the size of your business, you can still proactively connect with potential employees and develop your employer brand. If your company has a great story to tell and you put it across in an engaging way, you don't need recruitment agency budgets anymore – you can create interest in your organization with minimal spend. Unfortunately, despite this there are still far too many companies which see recruitment in a transactional, linear way, instead of building relationships and communities in *advance* of needing new staff.

What the smart recruiters do well

Clever companies know the traditional forms of recruiting aren't necessarily the best ways to access top talent, so they do four things excellently. You'll also see as you go through these how they treat their recruits as adults, consumers, and human beings at the same time.

Smart recruiters create an ultra-desirable employer brand

Social media and digital platforms have changed everything. They can build or tear down employer reputations in a matter of hours, as the famous 'United Breaks Guitars' video[1] shows. If you've not watched this it's well worth a few minutes of your time on YouTube, as it's a powerful example of how individuals have the ability to make or break company reputations if they understand how to use social media. In this case a musician was distraught to discover United Airlines had damaged his beloved guitar, so he wrote a song about it, recorded it, and put it on YouTube. It tells the sorry tale of how his guitar was broken by baggage handlers' apparently throwing it onto the plane, and of the obstructive and unhelpful responses of United customer service staff who refused to compensate him. The video shows mocked-up 'footage' of the handlers laughing as they swing the guitar around and the service staff pouting with boredom in response to his complaints. The most popular version of it on YouTube has over 15 million views.

Of course the main aim of the video was to damage the airline's brand reputation, but what did it do to its employer reputation at the same time? The employees are portrayed as unprofessional, unmotivated, and lazy – surely a terrible blow to the ability to attract the best talent to the organization.

This example highlights something companies are increasingly waking up to: potential employees are constantly checking out the reputation of corporations online. Glassdoor has 600,000 businesses on its database, which means anonymous comments from employees about their experiences, pay, and managers provide a warts-and-all picture of a company. Of course, the reason we trust platforms like TripAdvisor for advice is because we believe our peers will give a more honest opinion than the company we're handing over our money to. Your organization can pump all the cash it likes into job adverts and recruitment agencies, but what savvy employees are actually doing is looking at what other employees of your company (and your customers) are already saying about you. This means, in the same way your marketing department monitors what consumers say about your organization, you also need to know what people think about you as an employer.

As a great example of how to manage this, Glenn Elliott, CEO of Reward Gateway, an employer benefits company in the US, has recently committed to personally responding to every Glassdoor review within 24 hours. He knows it's not just the employee feedback that's important, but also how it's dealt with. In contrast, a particular law firm listed on Glassdoor (which shall remain nameless) had a slew of terrible reviews: 'deceptive', 'unethical', 'poorly managed', 'working here is psychological torture', 'for the love of God don't work here' – the list goes on. Its CEO, instead of taking on board the issues and trying to do something about them, tried to sue. Thus proving them right!

LinkedIn produced some great research not too long ago that discovered that 75% of candidates will research a company's reputation before applying and that nearly 70% of candidates wouldn't accept a job somewhere with a bad reputation even if they were unemployed at the time.[2]

The current crisis has really polarized companies into those who have behaved ethically towards their staff and those who have behaved appallingly. For every company that aimed to protect jobs and provided amazing support to its people during lockdown, there was the opposite end of the ethical spectrum with staff being laid off via Zoom. How our company behaves during the crisis will shape our employment brand for years to come.

What this all shows is your reputation as an employer brand is incredibly important, but the way you build it up isn't by having a lot of glossy brochures or adverts – it's through your current employees. There are three things you can do here.

- Encourage your employees to speak out. By allowing your staff to speak freely you're showing you trust them, and you're therefore more likely to generate more positive comments than negative ones. Starbucks does a really good job of building its brand through its employees. Starbucks has a @StarbucksJobs Instagram and Twitter account that it uses specifically to promote its employer brand and interact with potential candidates. It uses the hashtag #sbuxjobschat to encourage people to contribute feedback and also regularly posts links to its LinkedIn and other social media pages for easy access to resources.
- Ask your people what it's like to work in your company and use their testimonials online. For this very reason, one organization I'm working with is actively asking its people to put their views on Glassdoor.
- Ensure every employee is armed with a brand message about your organization.

Smart recruiters cut through the noise

What's the second thing smart recruiters do well? They use innovative marketing techniques to differentiate themselves from all the other companies going after the same talent.

You might ask if this is anything new – after all, companies have always competed for the best people. So why is it in most businesses the marketing and HR teams behave as if they're on different planets? Marketers are absolutely brilliant at understanding how to exploit the communication channels available to them, how to convey a message in a succinct and persuasive way, and how to tell a brand story, but rarely does HR tap into this expertise. It's true, recruitment is hardly the sexy stuff of marketing managers' dreams, and I don't often see these same managers beating down the HR department's door demanding to be let in. But HR can be equally guilty of assuming marketing is all smoke and mirrors. As we know, in our disrupted world, working across boundaries is not always easy – but that doesn't mean we shouldn't be doing it.

There's a view among some senior marketing specialists that it's now time to completely hand over the advertising, promotional, and branding element of recruitment to them. And why not? What department could possibly be better placed to help an organization create an employer brand, communicate it effectively, and persuade potential recruits to apply for roles than marketing? In fact other companies have also taken a marketing approach to recruitment and I'd like to share some exciting and innovative examples with you.

You may have seen the Heineken 'Candidate' video[3] in which various unsuspecting applicants are filmed going through the job interview process. Only it's not the kind of procedure anyone would be familiar with; they're tested in a series of bizarre ways. I won't spoil it for you by giving away the emotional climax, but the film leaves the viewer thinking about what kind of person Heineken wants. And yes, it looks expensive, but there would be many ways of achieving similar results for a lower cost.

Gamification is an increasingly popular trend in recruitment advertising. Microsoft created a challenging recruitment ad headed 'Problem solvers wanted. Call us on this number now'. But instead of giving a phone number it showed an equation which had to be cracked before the number would reveal itself; those looking for an easy job opening were soon discouraged. KPMG developed an online game based on the theme of 'around the world in 80 days'. Graduates had to fly a balloon around the world and complete ten challenges along the way; the fastest one received £1,000 of travel vouchers and a two-week internship at KPMG. Even those who weren't successful would have felt great about the company for giving them a fun experience. Marriott created an excellent recruitment campaign to attract potential employees – using an online game entitled My Marriott Hotel. It was created with the intent to encourage young people to take an interest in hospitality as a career path. The virtual game is much like Farmville or The Sims, requiring candidates to demonstrate their skills in a fun, online environment. It was a social media success that drove traffic to the company's Facebook career page. Because of this gamification trend over 70% of Forbes Global 2000 companies plan to use gamification in their recruitment from now on.

I'm also seeing a huge increase in the use of social media for recruitment; we all know about LinkedIn, Facebook, and Twitter, but the use of Snapchat (the instant messaging app which allows users to send photos and messages) is also on the rise. Norwegian advertising agency DBB Oslo[4] created a student competition in which candidates had to pitch their best ideas in ten seconds on Snapchat. This resulted in over 700 ideas from fresh, creative talent, with the films being watched over 50,000 times on YouTube and Vimeo. The agency's creative department viewed every single one. The benefit to the company was not only an outstanding recruit, but also the ideas it gained and the extra social media followers (with whom it could then keep in touch for future recruitment).

If you're not yet convinced of the value in your marketing department taking control of your recruitment campaigns, I hope you're at least thinking about it. The key is to create content your target audience finds enjoyable, because if your video features a guy in a grey suit talking about how innovative and interesting your company is, that's not going to wash. Your employer brand has to cut through the noise so it grabs the attention of the people you want to attract.

Smart recruiters target the key talent

The third thing smart recruiters do well is proactively target the talent they want, rather than wait for it to come to them.

Traditionally, if we want someone special we go to an expensive recruitment agent who opens up his or her little black book (for a fee) and approaches the person on our behalf. But nowadays social media has made this relatively easy for us to do ourselves, so if we know how to search for the right people online we can avoid the wastage of interviewing and then rejecting a series of candidates. Not only does this save us a hell of a lot of time, it also means we can avoid making the 'rejects' feel bad (they're our potential customers and referral agents, after all).

US-based game development company Red 5 Studios[5] needs, as you can imagine, to attract the best game developers around. To do this on one occasion it identified the top 100 people in this field and sent them an engraved iPod containing a personalized recorded message from the CEO. How's that for treating your potential employees as consumers? Even if you were really happy with your current employer, this kind of approach from another company would at least prompt a phone call. You might think this would be expensive, but what is getting the right people worth to you? And it doesn't have to be an iPod – how about a handwritten note or a small gift? It's the personal treatment that makes it special.

Targeting effectively is also about finding your candidates in non-traditional places where they actually hang out. Goldman Sachs uses Spotify to advertise vacancies, for example, and Amazon has even used Tinder!

Smart recruiters build a community of willing potential employees

The final thing the best recruiters do well is build long-term communities of potential recruits, to which interested people can invite themselves. In the traditional, linear recruitment world, candidates are invited to apply for a specific role and if they're not suitable they're rejected, never to be seen again. In this new world, companies are recognizing they need to build long-term relationships with the folk who might *one day* work for them, not just with their consumers.

So what does it mean to build a community of potential employees? Let's look at a couple of great examples. The first is online shoe retailer Zappos (you wouldn't expect a chapter on innovative recruitment not to include them, would you?). In 2013 it worked out it'd received 31,000 applications, of which 350 resulted in new hires, which meant it'd sent out 30,650 rejection letters. That took up a disproportionate amount of its time and meant it'd disappointed a huge number of people, many of whom were probably also its customers. As a result it developed the Insider Program, in which it completely abandoned job postings to focus instead on creating a community of future prospects. Each Insider who joins uploads his or her CV, fills out a brief questionnaire, and is then assigned to an 'ambassador' (one of Zappos' recruiters), who stays in touch with the Insider.

Take a look at Zappos' recruitment Twitter account @InsideZappos to see the friendly and proactive way the company communicates with its pool of potential recruits. What's most interesting, and unusual for a large company's recruiter account, is that it follows back almost as many people as follow it. Zappos doesn't use its social media as a broadcast tool but as an engagement device, to show it's as interested in what its followers say as in what it has to say to its followers. Not only is this a brilliant way of filtering out the less interested potential employees, but I'm sure it costs Zappos a lot less than expensive advertising campaigns or recruitment agencies.

Whereas Zappos is building relationships with people before they come to work with it, DaVita, the US healthcare provider, is using previous employees as a source of new recruits *after they've left*. The company's philosophy is: 'once a team mate, always a team mate, and you'll always have your own special place in the village'. In 2013 these 'boomerang' employees made up 15% of its hires. That might seem a little unusual, but if someone has worked for you in the past why wouldn't you want them to come back? If you've stayed in touch with them you'll be familiar with what they're up to and whether you'd want them to return. They know you, you know them, and if they've actively decided to join your 'alumni association' they must feel they've got a good relationship with you. They're also under no illusions about what it's like to work for you (a mismatch of expectations is one of the key reasons people leave).

This is all exciting and innovative, but unfortunately most recruitment advertising is still incredibly dull; when I look at the recruitment pages of company websites I'm rarely left with the feeling I'd like to work there. Creating a desirable employer brand, cutting through the noise, targeting key talent by means of personalization, and developing a community – that's the direction in which recruitment advertising is moving now.

The assessment process

The second part of the recruitment process is assessing for the job the candidates we've attracted. This is an area in which HR has made less progress, with poor interview techniques and a lack of imagination around discovering what makes someone perfect for a role being the norm. I've accompanied hiring managers who flicked through the CV while walking to the interview, didn't make eye contact with the interviewee, and talked at the interviewee for an hour without asking him any searching questions.

It doesn't stop there. Once the job is offered the feedback we give is typically extremely poor. Given an applicant has researched the job role and the organization, filled in the application, taken time out of her day to attend the interview, and gone through the nerve-wracking process of being grilled within an inch of her life, the least we can do is give this person decent feedback on why she didn't get the job. 'You weren't dynamic enough' isn't a sufficient response. When I was unsuccessful in gaining a job, being told why in detail made me feel warm towards the company. Unfortunately we still tend to process people through our recruitment system as if they were machines.

Successful consumer organizations would never do this to their customers. A supermarket, for instance, will separate the various elements of its customer experience into steps: what does it feel like to walk through the door? Who's the first person you meet? What's the layout like? What do you notice when you leave? How is the follow-up handled? It should be the same for recruitment. Our candidates go on a journey during which they'll experience our organization in various ways, and we want each touchpoint to be a positive one so that even if they don't get the job, they'll be telling their friends how well they were treated.

How to select (and not to select) your candidate

A lot of companies use competency-based interviewing techniques to choose the best applicant. As I'm sure you know, in the 1980s and 1990s HR departments went through agonies breaking down every job into competencies so people could be interviewed against them. There's no doubt this led to a higher degree of success in recruiting competent people, but there were (and still are) two main problems with them.

- They can be manipulated by applicants who are well practised in the process.
- More importantly, they're not suitable for discovering what a candidate loves doing and is truly talented at.

Clearly skills and competencies can't be ignored, especially in fields in which professional qualifications are essential. But there's an increasing, and exciting, trend towards assessment processes which enable us to get to know the applicants as people, discover their passions, feel what kind of energy they have, and learn what they're great at. Then we can work out how to use those talents rather than trying to shoe-horn employees into jobs in which they're good at seven out of the ten criteria we're assessing them against.

Reward consultancy organization NextJump has a great technique for doing this. It spent years examining which of its employees it would clone if it could, so it could structure their needs around a set of attributes rather than competencies. It eventually found its surest indicator of success was having a sense of humility. The ability to be open to other people's ideas was so important to it that it developed a 45-minute interview dedicated solely to finding out the applicant's propensity for humility, and anyone who didn't measure up wasn't hired. It also looked at three other areas: gratefulness versus entitlement, responsibility for one's own actions rather than feeling like a victim of circumstance, and a willingness to invest in doing things outside of one's comfort zone rather than 'knowing it all'. Once it got this right, its staff turnover fell from 40% to 1%.[6]

Another example of a company focusing on personal attributes rather than skills and competencies is ATB, a Canadian financial services organization. Prior to changing its hiring methods it looked for a strong sales background in its candidates, but it found although this approach brought in short-term sales it didn't make the people successful within the company's culture. So it looked at its top performers and saw what each was doing was not 'being a good salesperson' but 'being someone who wanted to deeply understand their clients'. This led it to create a list of desirable attributes such as authenticity and the ability to connect to people and communicate well. Again, it experienced a huge reduction in staff turnover.

Aviva, the UK insurance company, has also started using strengths-based recruitment. It evaluated 60 different competencies, such as time management, teamwork, and empathy, which it then integrated into its interview methodology. This shifted its approach from assessing people's past performance to evaluating their future potential. As a result it's seen its staff productivity levels increase by

21%, delays in its call centres fall by 54%, customer satisfaction jump by 12%, employment churn halved in the first 12 months, and morale noticeably improve.[7]

RWE npower goes one step further and doesn't specify the role at all when it creates a job ad. Candidates are interviewed based on their soft skills and experience, not on their ability to manipulate their CVs for a specific role. Through this, its hiring managers gain a genuine insight into the applicants and are then able to recommend the right roles.

You can see the difference it makes when you focus on the person rather than the job, and if you think about it that's probably how you'd prefer it if it were you. I know I want to be chosen for who I am, for my passions and my energy, rather than for the list of experiences I can tick off.

So how can we recruit new employees more effectively?

To recruit well we need to see our potential employees as real people rather than as a set of skills to shoe-horn into job roles. Here's a key list of don'ts and dos.

The don'ts

- Don't focus only on the experience and competencies your recruit will need in the role.
- Don't see recruitment as a linear, transactional process where the company retains all control.

The do's

- Think about your employer brand and take active steps to develop a positive one.

- Be creative about how you promote your vacancies so you cut through the noise.
- Be personal when you target the people you want.
- Develop a two-way community of potential employees so you can draw on them when you need them.
- Focus on personal qualities rather than skills and experience when you evaluate your candidates.

Let's finish by looking at how implementing these changes around recruitment will help you treat your employees as adults, consumers, and human beings.

Adults

- Creating a community for people who are interested in your company allows potential employees to feel in control. It's their decision to participate.
- Trusting your employees to do the recruitment for you enables them to use their own authentic voice.

Consumers

- Tailoring your approaches to new talent according to their individual personalities means you're treating them as individuals.
- Paying attention to your company's employer brand shows you care about what your candidates think about you, as much as you care about what you think about them.
- Using a range of recruitment techniques such as video and gamification means you're appealing to different segments of your employee base.

Human beings

- Giving helpful feedback to rejected candidates (or only approaching the people you think you want, thereby avoiding rejecting people in the first place) affords the applicants dignity.

- Selecting on the basis of personal qualities rather than competencies brings the humanity back into your recruitment process.

- Treating the interview like a conversation, in which you build rapport so as to find out more about the candidate, involves treating them as a whole person.

7

Induction

I bet you remember your first day at your current company. You were probably aiming to make a mental note of where the toilets were and to find out the direction of the canteen, and trying like hell to remember all the names. 'This is Kathy, she looks after all our procedures. And here's Ben, the office crazy guy (eh, Ben?).' It was pretty bewildering, wasn't it? The colleagues who made you feel at home you'll be forever grateful to; the grumpy one who didn't bother to smile is still on your avoid list. Every event during this critical period takes on an extra meaning, so although induction is a small part of your life cycle as an employee, it punches way above its weight.

Whether you call it induction (as we do in the UK) or onboarding (in the US), it means the same thing – it's all about how we get new employees bedded in and working effectively as quickly as possible. Or so we think. A friend of mine recently joined a large corporate organization; I asked him how his first week had gone and he replied, 'Oh, you know, induction hell.' What a shame he had the typical, shabby experience.

Let's analyze what we do when we induct new employees. Do we make them feel welcomed, valued, and excited about being part of our enterprise? Do we treat them as individuals with their own backgrounds, preferences, and personalities? No, we put them through a one-size-fits-all sausage machine. Usually this involves some kind of death-by-PowerPoint experience crammed with bullet points from all the departments which have managed to crowbar their way onto it, a cursory tour around the offices, and finally the ceremonial signing of countless pieces of paperwork. Welcome to our organization!

The entire process is geared towards encouraging conformity: 'Don't imagine your individuality or creativity is valued here', it says. Rarely does it make people feel special or celebrate the fact they're joining the company. Going back to how we all felt when we started at our places of work, what mattered most to us on the first day was getting to know whom we were working with, finding out where the coffee machine was, and identifying that one person in the department who always seems to know where everything is kept. And yet our induction processes ignore these simple, human needs and focus instead on the company's expectations of the new recruit.

Recently I helped one of the top-four accountancy firms redesign its induction process, and in doing so carried out some research with 15 of its graduates who'd joined a few years earlier. I asked them to think back along their entire induction experience, from the moment they first got their offer letter through to when they actually started the job, and it was amazing to hear what they had to say. They'd been through a hell of a lot to actually get the position – gaining their degree, going through the gruelling assessment process – so when that letter of acceptance at a prestigious company finally arrived on their doormat they were ecstatic. How special and proud a moment that was for them; parents were phoned (possibly for the first time in weeks) and drinks were bought all round. And yet how quickly this joy dissipated once they were channelled through the sort of induction process I described above. A time which could have been incredibly positive, had they been given some consideration as individuals, was turned into a series of instructions about what the company wanted them to know. Of course there will always be things people have to be told when they join, but why don't we take as much care over how we want them to *feel*?

So what can we do differently?

Creating a more welcoming and useful induction process takes some imagination and creativity. You need to put yourself into the shoes of a new recruit and think about how you can make his first few days and weeks special. There's plenty of research out there that gives us the insights about what makes a great induction or onboarding experience. Great onboarding is all about:

- being manager-led; 72% of employees surveyed by enboarder[1] said one-on-one time with their direct manager is the most important aspect of any pre-boarding or onboarding process;
- creating a sense of belonging; 70 separate studies show that feeling socially accepted was a key factor in newcomer success. Of course, this can be even harder and more important without that physical contact if your employees are increasingly working from home;
- avoiding being all about the paperwork; it's vital that employees find it an engaging experience and so getting the admin out of the way before they start is essential; and
- being designed around and owned by the employee themselves; the more personal and customized you can make it, the better.

Here are some examples of companies that have really innovated in this area so you can use them as inspiration for generating your own ideas.

Bazaarvoice is a Texas-based tech company which runs a week-long scavenger hunt for recruits comprised of a series of tasks and questions the newbies have to find the answers to. The hunt takes them into all areas of the company – its structure, history, departments, and cultures. This means they see as much of the company, and meet as many people, as they can; it also enables the new recruits to find things out for themselves as adults instead of being spoon-fed information like children.

Employer Mum and Employer Dad sit new starters down and tell them about the company, but some organizations ask employees to induct each other. Southwest Airlines, for instance, invites people from all levels of the company to talk about their jobs to recruits. Whole Foods, the US grocery retailer, actually gets its employees (not the HR manager or the store manager) to decide whether a new starter should stay or not. After 90 days the team is invited to vote on whether to keep the employee; this sounds quite brutal but actually makes a lot of sense given they're the ones most likely to know if the person is right for the company. And a two-thirds majority is needed to vote someone out.[2]

Commerce Sciences, a Silicon Valley tech start-up, has a tradition in which the last person to join the team is responsible for creating a starter kit for the next person. This means each kit is different and personalized, and springs from the originator's creativity.[3] How different this is from the standard corporate information pack produced by HR because (of course!) HR knows what everyone needs.

Twitter has a 'Yes to desk' process involving numerous interactions with the employee before they even start to get the bureaucracy out of the way early.

Ernst & Young provides an innovative onboarding portal that includes an online virtual tour that provides its new hires with information about the firm, it walks them through the onboarding process, and it answers the questions that were most frequently asked by previous new hires.

MasterCard newbies receive a welcoming email which includes links to company videos, and access to a website where they can 'update their employment information, upload a photo for their badge, read about learning opportunities and complete paperwork'. The new hire's manager can also go online to select the tools and office space they will need, so everything will be ready for them on their first day.

Other companies are also finding ways to make new employees feel socially connected. At Bonobos, the US e-commerce clothing company, the hiring manager (not the HR manager) sends an email to the entire company introducing each new employee. This includes a brief biography and photo and also a trivia game called 'Two Truths and a Lie'. Only two of the three fun facts about the employee are true. In order to work out which is the lie the existing employees are encouraged to meet the person and find out, with the first to get to the truth receiving a $25 store credit. It means an enormous amount to new recruits to be actively welcomed into the organization; in this company the onus isn't on them to find out who everyone else is, but for everyone else to find out about them. It also encourages employees to behave as humans and adults together (ironically, through a childlike game).[4]

At Salesforce the company pairs every new hire with a 'Trail Guide', a peer mentor that helps them get oriented and makes their experience feel personal. The Trail Guide is a confidant that new hires go to for guidance, support, and any questions they may have along the way.

And there's more. Google's HR team sends an email to the hiring manager of a new recruit the day before he or she is due to start, reminding the manager of five things. There are no prescriptive rules when it comes to these things, and the manager owns the process, but the HR team reckons by doing this they reduce the time it takes for a new recruit to become fully productive by a month. So what are these five things?

- We want you to have a discussion about their role and responsibilities.
- We want you to match them with a buddy so there's always someone they can go and ask.
- We want you to help them build their own social network, because they'll perform better if they're well connected within the organization as quickly as possible.
- We want you to set up a check-in with them once a month for the first six months.
- We want you to encourage open discussion and dialogue with them from day one.[5]

Are you feeling a bit more inspired now? What initiatives could you create with your induction programme to integrate new employees into your company?

The probationary period

I always feel like groaning when I hear the word 'probation'; it's an awful term, conjuring up images of prisons and criminals rather than the welcoming of new employees into the firm. Of course, the probationary period originally came about because if a company wanted to ask someone to leave, they used to have to do this within the employee's first year (now two years). But do we really need to set a term? Why wait three or six months to sit down with a new person and have a conversation about how it's going? Surely a manager would know more quickly than that if he'd made a mistake by hiring him. Apart from anything else, it's so unwelcoming: 'Hello on your first day, we're so glad you joined us. But don't get too comfortable – you're on probation, and at the end of your probationary period you'll have a review in which we'll let you know whether you can stay or not. Feel free to be loyal to us in the meanwhile, though.' For one of the companies we've worked with on improving the employee welcoming process we've changed the name of the probationary period to the 'settling in' period, which is much more human. One airline we work with at Disruptive HR went even further. It looked back at how many people actually failed its probation period and found that it was around two people every year – out of a workforce of 10,000! It quickly dropped it and so when you start you don't have the sword of Damocles hanging over your head!

A business process outsourcing company in India has a great way of getting to know its new starters. It gives them a problem-solving exercise and encourages them to reflect on how they approached it. This helps both parties analyze the recruit's particular strengths, which leads to a discussion about how those abilities could be applied to their job. It's not expecting its recruits to conform to them – in fact, quite the opposite. It's seeking ways to adapt its approach so it can help its people bring their best selves to work. And the result of all this? It has a 33% higher retention rate in the first six months, and it's led to better customer satisfaction levels as well. How different this is from the one-size-fits-all approach most other companies adopt.

I couldn't end this chapter without talking about Zappos. Every year it offers its employees up to $5,000 to leave, with the express hope they'll not take up the offer but will recommit to the owner, Amazon, instead. The reason it does this is to encourage employees to reflect on why they work there, which creates a deeper sense of engagement. What a wonderful antidote to the notion of the employer holding all the cards.

So how can we welcome new employees into our organizations more effectively?

By imagining what it would be like to be new recruits in our own companies again, and by reflecting on our own experiences of starting in various organizations, we can see there is much we can change.

The don'ts

- Don't throw all the information your new starters will ever need at them in the first week.
- Don't do probationary periods.

The dos

- Think about the way you want your new recruits to feel rather than just about what you want them to know.
- Devise an induction process that acknowledges your unique culture and style of working.
- Put yourself in the starters' shoes and ask how you would feel if you were them.

Let's finish by looking at how implementing these changes around induction will help you treat your employees as adults, consumers, and human beings.

Adults

- Creating a two-way process in which they're encouraged to ask questions allows them to feel respected.
- Setting up the information so they can find it at the time they need it places the responsibility on them.
- Involving their peers avoids the top-down approach.

Consumers

- Tailoring inductions to different types of recruits makes the process more meaningful for them.
- Putting yourself in their shoes enables you to create a system which welcomes them into your firm.

Human beings

- Avoiding the sausage-machine approach makes new starters feel appreciated and motivated.
- Drip-feeding information takes account of how we operate as humans; we can't possibly retain all the information that's parcelled up for us on day one.

8

Employment rules and policies

My daughter Kate took up her first job after leaving university not long ago (with an employer that has a brilliant reputation for being caring), and she was excited when her joining pack landed on the doormat. But she was gutted when she tore it open only to find page upon page of policies for her to read and sign. Some of them even required her to initial each page to 'prove' she'd read them.

Who were they kidding? Did they really think a signature was evidence of her having read, absorbed, and understood every last element of them, especially given she hadn't even started working there yet? And what effect did they think this all had on her morale as a new starter? The first batch of information she received was written with the assumption she was going to do something wrong – what a fantastic way to begin a new career.

The employee handbook

My daughter's experience isn't untypical; the employee handbook is usually one of the first pieces of communication HR sends to new employees before they start.

'Welcome to our company. We're really excited to have you join us and we hope you're feeling the same. Oh, and by the way, here's a legal contract – we know there's a 1% chance you'll read it – and a handbook telling you all the things you're not allowed to do.'

There is another way. Increasingly, forward-thinking organizations keep their policies available in the background so people can read them if they want to but are not forced to digest and sign them. This is a sign of trust; their starting point is they expect their staff to behave well and treat the company and their colleagues with respect. Instead of sending the handbook to new starters they give them a 'Welcome Pack' filled with engaging information about the way the company works, its values and culture, which helps them make a lot more sense of the policies when/if they do get to read them.

As you'll know from Chapter 3 ('Employees as adults') I have a strong aversion to prescriptive HR rules and procedures, and in particular to those based on lowest-common-denominator behaviour. So I won't go into further detail on this here, but I'd like to share my thoughts on how you can do it better.

How to create a rule book that doesn't frustrate and annoy your people

I came across one company, Valve Software, which does this so well. Its handbook makes me feel like I'd love to work there; it talks about its approach to working and to colleague relationships in an open and honest way that's consistent with its brand and values. From the outset it encourages a sense of personal responsibility.[1] So how can you do something similar? There are three elements to this.

Trust your employees

Try answering this question about each of your policies: does this rule exist because we don't trust some of our people to do it properly? If your answer is yes, then the chances are you're patronizing and annoying a large number of valuable people in order to stop the odd rogue from doing something wrong. When I work with organizations that have rule books like this and ask them why they've drawn them up, they'll often say it's because a certain person overstepped the line once, or because they predicted it would be an area people would slip up on. This goes back to treating employees like children; we put in place safeguards to forestall any possible problem rather than robustly tackling the individual who's actually causing the issue. This tackling, of course, involves having a difficult conversation with the person, so the temptation is to write a policy as a way of abdicating that responsibility.

Encourage sensible judgement

At the BBC we decided to publish our senior managers' expense claims on our website. Understandably these managers were nervous because they knew they'd be scrutinized by the national media, and their fears were not unfounded. But what was most interesting was that although there was the expected criticism of the costs incurred in expensive flights and taxis, the main thing that upset both more junior employees and the general public was the pettiness of the claims for everyday items. Here were directors who earned hundreds of thousands of pounds a year seemingly not able to pay for their own second-class stamps or coffee.

What happened next? It was proposed we needed to revamp our expenses policy and put it in our staff handbook, to keep our managers 'safe' from that kind of spending. I was appalled by this because the logical extension of that argument would be that HR should decide what items a manager could claim, with the document potentially going on ad infinitum. I've already praised Netflix's expenses policy, which consists of just a few words: 'Act in Netflix's best interest'. Surely we should be able to trust intelligent people to claim appropriately? And if we can't, what does that say about both our culture and their outlook?

So, replacing long-winded policies that try to cover every eventuality with a simple statement that encourages people to use their judgement not only places the responsibility on everyone to behave in the right way, but also takes a load off HR's shoulders. By doing this you avoid frustrating the people who would naturally do the right thing and you encourage the use of good judgement on a day-to-day basis in all areas of work.

Write your policies from your employees' perspective

When we write our policies for the lowest common denominator we infantilize our staff. We need people to be able to think for themselves, not feel they have to go to a manual every time they have a decision to make. Instead, if we ask our employees what they wish they'd known when they started and use that as a starting point for the handbook, the chances are we'll create one that's useful, well loved, and frequently referenced.

Clothing retailer Gap has a great approach to its social media policy. It knows it needs to moderate its employees' social media use, but it also doesn't want to treat them like children. Its approach is interesting as the policy's style is conversational but also to the point. Here are some excerpts.

1. **Some subjects can invite a flame war.** Be careful discussing things where emotions run high (e.g., politics and religion) and show respect for others' opinions.

2. **Your job comes first.** Unless you are an authorized social media manager, don't let social media affect your job performance.

3. **If you #!%#@# up?** Correct it immediately and be clear about what you've done to fix it. Contact the social media team if it's a real doozy.

4. **Don't even think about it...** Talking about financial information, sales trends, strategies, forecasts, legal issues, future promotional activities. Giving out personal information about customers or employees. Posting confidential or non-public information. Responding to an offensive or negative post by a customer. There's no winner in that game.[2]

If I were one of Gap's employees, at no point would I feel patronized, belittled, or irritated by this policy; I'd just feel I had a clear sense of what was acceptable and what wasn't, and that it was up to me to use my judgement.

But what if...?

Of course, we live in a litigious society so we can't pretend we don't need any guidelines at all, lovely though that might be. I'm not an advocate of chaos or anarchy in the workplace. And I do believe that some areas are more likely to require strong instructions in order to avoid exposing an organization to legal action. But

I also think that as soon as anyone starts having to refer to the contract or the guidelines in a situation at work, then we've already reached a difficult place. It's far better to encourage a culture of responsibility and ownership in the first place so we don't have to reach for the legal documents every time something goes wrong. How much better would it be to make the values and the ethos of the organization clear so we can make up our own minds about how to act?

The benefit of this is not just huge time-saving for HR, or even that HR can move out of the role of compliance officer. It's also the fact that all employees will feel trusted to use their judgement, comfortable with challenging the status quo, and encouraged to find things out for themselves – and they will be more productive. Increased morale, innovation, and creativity are ample rewards for taking the odd risk with your policies.

So how can we create rules and policies that work for everyone?

One document can never cater to every person's needs, but if you start from the point of the mid-range denominator (rather than the bottom), you won't go far wrong. Here are some pointers.

The don'ts

- Don't write every policy for the rogue employee you expect to behave badly.
- Don't rush to write or amend a policy when something goes wrong; instead, ask yourself what it is about your culture (or about the offending employee) that's caused the problem.

The dos

- Write all your rules and policies from a position of trust.
- Encourage the use of good judgement when you advise your staff what parameters to work within.
- Think how you would feel if you were to read your policies for the first time.
- When an employee messes up, deal with him or her, not the rule book.

Let's finish by looking at how implementing these changes around rules and policies will help you treat your employees as adults, consumers, and human beings.

Adults

- Trusting your staff to make sensible judgements based on broad criteria avoids their feeling patronized.

Consumers

- Encouraging the individual interpretation of policies allows employees to make up their own minds.
- Writing your handbook from the perspective of your people means you're treating them like consumers.

Human beings

- Removing an unrealistically long list of procedures and policies which have to be read and signed means you're recognizing it's impossible for anyone to absorb that amount of information.

- Providing information on a 'need-to-know' basis encourages its use when it's necessary, not when HR thinks it should be read.

9

Managing performance

From the numerous conversations I have with HR managers who attend our Disruptive HR workshops and webinars, I pretty much know what the answer would be if I were to ask you which part of HR you're most convinced isn't working: performance management. I'm specifically talking about annual appraisals. Managers hate them, employees hate them, and HR gets frustrated with them.

So what's wrong with appraisals? I've been known to rant about this on more than one occasion, but for your sake I'll keep it as brief as possible and explain why we should rid ourselves of appraisals and replace them with something much more effective.

First of all there's the huge amount of time and effort that goes into them. At the BBC we'd start discussing annual objectives at a strategic level in November so they could be debated, discussed, agreed upon, and signed off by March. Managers would then be required to squeeze in a dozen appraisals with their team members, taking two to three hours per person (including preparation time). This all had to be done within a month's timescale, with the result that the whole organization became so focused on appraisals there was little time for anything else.

This time-suck of management hours is expensive. When Deloitte looked at how much it spent on annual appraisals, it found it was 2 million hours globally.[1] In terms of how much these appraisals cost in people hours I've found only one organization which has estimated this, and the number is £1,500 per employee. That's a huge amount of time and money being poured into a system that doesn't work.

Having said all this, I realize behind appraisals lies good intent; we want to help our employees to be clear on their goals and how their performance contributes to their organization's success. It feels good to create a process in which feedback is given and staff are helped to improve, doesn't it? Unfortunately, the system's taken over and we've become slaves to it. Instead of appraisals being about raising ambition, clarifying contribution, coaching people, and having mutually beneficial conversations (in other words, being human), they're now embedded within a system that mainly exists to generate a rating which decides people's bonuses.

I've already mentioned the research that shows 92% of companies have an annual appraisal but only 8% really believe they're worth the time and effort devoted to them. Furthermore, it seems around 70% of companies are already thinking about changing them but haven't yet found a better way of managing performance. We all know the saying about the definition of madness being doing the same thing over and over but expecting a different result. To me, this insistence on keeping our broken annual appraisal system is the definition of corporate insanity. In all my years in HR I've never met a manager who enjoys giving an appraisal. And we know that if we don't enjoy doing something or feel there's a point to it, we don't throw ourselves into it wholeheartedly.

The vast majority of employees I talk to see appraisals as hoops to jump through in order to get a rating or grade which will mark them as good, bad, or incompetent.

How demotivating is that? And HR justifies it on the basis of needing a fair, transparent, and equitable way to distribute bonuses. It's HR neatness again! What's more, because we can guarantee these conversations will be happening each year, we've loaded them with all sorts of extra 'stuff'. They're used not only to set objectives and improve performance, but also to discuss training and development, look at careers, and distribute rewards. The system is creaking under the weight.

So why do we remain wedded to the annual appraisal process? I believe there are two main reasons.

- **We've been doing them for so long we can't imagine an alternative.** We've taken decades to invent this process and still more decades to embed it. There are also countless HR guides from the 1980s and 1990s telling us appraisals improve performance, and we don't really have any hard evidence they don't. We can just see with our own eyes, and feel intuitively, they're not a useful tool.
- **We don't know what else to do.** Better the devil you know, right? Even though our current system is painful it does enable us to measure the input. So our boards and executive teams can say, for instance, 80% of their employees have had a performance conversation because they've got the form to prove it. We feel safer sticking with what we know than taking a risk with something new.

Let's be clear – this isn't all HR's fault. We've inherited a system which is a nightmare to dismantle because so much rides on it. So where do we go from here? As is the case when it comes to all major change, we need to be completely convinced of the wrongness of the old and familiar in order to feel bold enough to embrace the new and uncertain, so my next task is to convince you of the need for an alternative. At the end of this chapter I'll explain what you can do to create a more effective performance management environment.

The four great myths of annual appraisals

I'll come clean: I originally fell for these same myths as an HR director. I'm not going to pretend I had all the answers then, and it certainly took until quite recently for me to see through them. But since then I've done my research and now feel completely confident I can bust each myth in turn.

Myth 1: Annual objectives provide clarity and a focus for ambition

There are a number of reasons why this isn't so.

The first is most companies tend to lumber people with too many different types of objectives. A single person can end up with a harvest of her own objectives, her broader team objectives, her departmental objectives, and even her organizational objectives. While we're at it, why not throw in a CSR objective, a diversity objective, and a health and safety objective or two? One poor guy I spoke to at the BBC told me he had a whopping total of 85 objectives. Clearly this was an extreme case, but I could see how it had happened. He'd got his global BBC objectives, BBC News objectives, BBC Regional News objectives, local radio station objectives, a people objective, a safety objective, a finance objective – the list goes on. It's utterly crazy. The reason this happens is managers see objectives as a mechanism for driving the changes they want. If the diversity team, for example, wants to meet a particular goal that year they'll ask for it to be tied into people's objectives. Let's add in a diversity objective! But the reality is if each employee has 20 or 30 objectives, adding in a diversity goal isn't going to focus their minds on that area one bit.

There's also the bottom-drawer syndrome: people forget about their objectives. Come annual appraisal time how often do you take calls from a stream of managers and employees asking you if you've got a copy of their objectives from last year because they can't find them? We labour under the illusion if somebody's got an objective it's going to be front of mind, but it's not. This leads to another reason, which is that in a fast-moving world the notion of setting an objective in April that's still going to be relevant the following March is absurd. If the last year has taught us anything, it's that we can't possibly predict with any accuracy how the next 12 months will unfold. I don't think I've ever looked at my objectives at the year end and felt they were still key to my role. They need to change all the time to accommodate the fluid nature of our work and the changing world around us.

As well, we work in teams. Even the most sophisticated manager struggles to make the objectives he sets for his individuals greater than the sum of their parts. So team members end up with different sets of goals and therefore aren't focused on delivering excellent work through the groups they're in. Part of the reason for the lack of team objectives is the way we've historically attached annual bonuses to their achievement. It's hard to work out whether an individual person should receive a personal bonus when much of her work has been team-based.

Nor do objectives take into account human nature; it's back to treating employees as objects instead of human beings. Think about when you want to get fit. You don't want to go to the gym, lose weight, and stop drinking because someone tells you to – you want to decide for yourself. It's the same with objectives; a 'want to' goal is always going to be easier to reach than a 'have to' goal.

And finally, the attachment of bonuses to objectives is actually a driver of mediocrity rather than excellence; who wouldn't want to negotiate down on their goals so they're more achievable when their holiday abroad this year might depend on it?

I hope by now you're joining me in questioning the purpose of this bureaucratic, time-rich, and costly exercise. Managing performance should improve productivity and motivation, but I don't see the annual goal-setting process doing this.

Myth 2: Feedback drives improved performance

If feedback is given brilliantly it can improve performance. But as we know, the annual appraisal system is far from brilliant. Why doesn't it work as a feedback mechanism?

The first reason goes back to the parent–child dynamic so prevalent in HR. In a typical appraisal session, two adults sit together but only one has the form to fill in and makes the judgements. When I ask people how they feel about being on the receiving end of this, they tell me it's like being back at school. In Chapter 5 ('Employees as human beings'), I explained Dr David Rock's findings on what happens when we feel threatened: the part of our brain that solves problems, thinks laterally, and is open to feedback shuts down. So at the very moment when we want people to be most interested in how they can improve their performance, they throw up their defences. All they're thinking is, 'What rating am I going to get at the end of this? What will they say about me? Will I like it or not?' This means instead of being happy to have an open conversation about how they could do better, they're more likely to go into a sulky, defensive, and childlike mode.

The second part of this myth about feedback is what I call the recency syndrome. Most managers find it difficult to remember what someone's performance has been over an entire year. So the feedback they give tends to relate to employees' most recent behaviour, whereas the appraisal is supposed to encompass a much longer time period than that.

What's more, as Dr David Rock also says, we're only really able to change one behaviour at a time, and we need feedback about it at the *moment that behaviour is evidenced*. It also needs to be consistently given over a period of around six weeks. What do we do in appraisals, though? We store up our feedback, expecting the employee to change seven or eight habits at once – habits that are out of context as well. It's impossible for any of us to improve our performance this way.

I also have concerns about who gives feedback to whom. In the first chapter I mentioned the millennial generation, which first came into the workplace around 2000. It's been suggested they don't value hierarchical feedback as much as previous generations; they're more interested in what their peers think of them than their managers. Facebook, for example, has moved from top-down to peer reviews because it's found them to be a better way of improving performance.

Myth 3: Appraisals provide objective and fair measurement

In HR we tie ourselves up in knots ensuring each appraisal results in a rating that's objective and transparent. Should we have an even number of boxes or an odd number? How about the language – does 'average' sound too judgemental or should we use 'meets expectations' instead? What on earth is the purpose of this tortuous process? Is it supposed to be motivational for the person on the receiving end to be told she 'meets expectations'? Can it possibly drive better performance?

Rankings and ratings are evident in their worst form in the system known as forced rank distribution. In case you're not familiar with this, it's a phenomenon that started in the 1980s which taps into the idea we need to force managers to be ruthless about weeding out poorly performing employees. All staff are ranked on a distribution curve, and some companies routinely fire those in the lower percentile. Terrible though this is, I couldn't help but smile when I discovered during a conversation with an HR director in the civil service that even within this aggressive system, human nature can still triumph. She told me she'd seen many close teams of people share the lowest rating amongst themselves so no one would get it two years in a row (the point at which they would be sacked). Humanity rules, okay!

Joking aside, there are some appalling consequences of forced rank or guided distribution. For a start, it's hugely demotivating and potentially unfair. It also encourages managers to abdicate responsibility for assessing their staff: 'If it were up to me I'd be giving you a top rating, but I've only got three this year and I gave you one last year, so this year you'll have to do without.' And finally, it creates a toxic culture in which for one person to win someone else has to lose. Although Microsoft moved away from forced rank distribution a number of years ago, its chief executive put a significant part of the company's 'lost decade' against Apple down to individual bonuses linked to this system.[2]

We also rate people with 360-degree feedback, and it's become increasingly popular as a way of achieving the ever-elusive goal of fair measurement. Done well as part of a development programme it can be incredibly helpful, but as part of the typical annual appraisal process it's a nightmare. Once a year any given senior manager will receive countless requests to fill in 360s. The problem is, I know from personal experience how hard it can be to fairly rate someone I don't know that well; although I always intended to do a fair and thorough job, I know I rarely did that in reality. Then, when the employee on the receiving end of the assessment reads the comments, there are usually two types she'll pay attention to: the ones she's already heard (so what's the point?), and the anonymous, negative comment. The impact of this can be severe.

Marcus Buckingham is a well-known assessment and measurement processes analyst, and his research has shown we're notoriously bad at judging other people objectively. According to him, 61% of our assessment of others is about us and 39% is about the other person. Of course, there's still value in our judgements, but if that's the only measurement employees get at the end of the year the phenomenon of the 'idiosyncratic rater effect' can distort the picture.[3]

Let's think about what this means in reality. During her appraisal, an employee can be happy to talk about how she could improve, but at the end of the conversation her manager will say, 'Right, so having talked about this I'm going to rate you a two.' I've seen the disappointment in people's eyes so often when I've done this; they were hoping for a one, or maybe they'd always had a one before so they felt entitled to it. I had a member of staff who was outstanding, but every year she'd come into her appraisal anxious and agitated; she said it was because of the number she was going to be marked with at the end. We have this crazy situation in which a number has so much power, and yet surely the value lies in the *conversation* not in the grading.

I've seen no evidence that giving someone a rating improves his performance or productivity one iota. In fact, a top accountancy firm looked at its ratings over a five-year period and found over 75% of its staff had been given the same rating year in, year out; all this did was drive a sense of entitlement to it.

And I keep coming back to the same questions: what is this trying to achieve? Do people feel more motivated and productive as a result? Why bother going through this at all?

Myth 4: Appraisals are needed for poor performers

When I talk to HR directors about how we can do performance management in a more adult-to-adult and humane way, most of them get where I'm coming from pretty quickly. There's one myth, however, they find it hard to stop believing in. 'But Lucy', they say, 'we need an annual appraisal because how else do we identify and deal with the poor performers?' I'm always amazed by this, because what they seem to be saying is they're happy to put 98% of their people through a process which demotivates them, doesn't drive value, and doesn't improve performance because they want to get to the 2% of people who behave badly. Doesn't that seem absurd?

But even leaving that point to one side, the fact is most managers find it incredibly difficult to record poor feedback on an appraisal form. They just don't do it. In my workshops I'm often joined by a senior partner in an employment law firm; I ask him to stand up and state his experience in this area. It can be summed up in one powerful sentence: 'You know, for 20 years I've been a senior partner in a law firm working on unfair dismissal tribunals, and in not one of them has an appraisal form ever helped an employer's case.' This makes sense. How many times have you tried to help a manager who was sick of one of his staff letting him down, only to look at the employee's appraisal form and find the person has been thanked for another great year? So I'm afraid the idea we need appraisals to deal with poor performance is just another myth.

How to manage performance without ratings and annual appraisals

There are two parts to what we can do instead; one is to find ways of rewarding people with individual bonuses without rating them, and the other is to explore how we can move away from annual appraisals altogether.

How to reward people with individual bonuses without rating them

'I get why rating people doesn't work and I'd love to get rid of ratings altogether. But how can I do so, when we have to retain an individual performance bonus? If we have a grade or a rating, we have a transparent way of distributing it which is seen as fair.' This is a common objection when I talk about doing away with performance ratings, and I understand the concern.

In the next chapter, on reward, I'll make a convincing case for why individual bonuses don't work either, but I also appreciate this can be the hardest element of performance management to give up as it's so embedded in our corporate culture. Therefore, if you want to stop the nonsense of rating people annually but still want to provide individuals with a bonus that rewards their personal contribution, you have three options.

- **A continuous assessment process.** This works well for organizations with regular performance periods such as monthly sales reviews or regular projects – consultancy firms are a good example. By assessing their people regularly they avoid the need for a grading at the end of the year and can distribute the bonus at the end of each period. For many companies, however, this can be even more onerous than the once-a-year performance assessment, so it's not for everyone.

- **An end-of-year 'contribution calibration' in which line managers agree who deserves what bonus.** Instead of the traditional calibration session in which managers debate who deserves what grade, they agree what bonus each person should receive relative to one another. The upside of this can be some good-quality conversations about people, and a challenge to those managers who use the bonus as a means of abdicating their development responsibilities. It can, however, be seen as unfair and lacking transparency by those in receipt of the outcome, especially if quality conversations about performance haven't taken place throughout the year.

- **Line manager discretion.** This allows managers total freedom for distributing bonuses to their people within a capped budget, and is currently the option that most companies which get rid of ratings, but want to keep individual bonuses, favour. If there's regular feedback between managers and their people throughout the year, and the bonus is simply an extension of those discussions and is therefore expected, this approach can work. But if these conversations don't exist the bonus can seem unfair, leading to accusations of favouritism and even discrimination. It's still early days in the abolition of the ratings trend, so it will be interesting to see whether this starts to get any pushback from disgruntled employees.

In truth, there's no foolproof way of getting rid of ratings and keeping individual performance bonuses. Every option requires a high level of management maturity and effective ongoing discussions during the year.

How to move away from annual appraisals altogether

First of all, please don't replace one standardized process with another. We're all different from each other; what motivates me won't necessarily motivate you, so the key to effectively managing performance is to individualize and customize as much as you can. Below are some alternative ideas for managing your employees' performance in an adult-to-adult, personalized, and humane way.

- Set team objectives instead of individual ones. We routinely deliver and work through teams rather than as a set of disparate individuals. Some companies are experimenting with setting team-based goals and reviewing the whole team's progress, with good results.
- Refresh objectives regularly. Deloitte has found organizations which renew their objectives quarterly have a higher share price and performance rating than other companies.
- Tell your staff it's up to them to take ownership of their performance. Increasingly companies are saying to new recruits, 'It's your responsibility to have conversations about your performance with your manager, and if you're not doing that we

want to know why.' Adobe is one such organization implementing an adult-to-adult policy in this way.[4]

- Develop the habit of having regular check-ins instead of an annual review, and recognize that managing performance is about having different types of conversations at various points in the year. They don't have to be formal meetings – they can be conversations by the water cooler or in the corridor as you leave a meeting. How about going over to someone's desk and telling her the way she just handled something was fantastic, or asking if you could look at a problem together and find a solution? This is a hard habit to instil but is effective and workable. IT company Atlassian has moved towards real-time coaching for its managers and leaders, as well as abandoning ratings in favour of establishing how often an individual has shown exceptional performance.[5]

- Enable your leaders to work as coaches so they're able to help their people improve performance on the job. Show them how different types of performance conversations can be done well.

- Develop a range of feedback mechanisms. Move away from a top-down approach towards feedback as a team, in which the team leader is not the 'grown-up' but an equal participant. I was fascinated to observe the BBC's *News at Ten* team members coming together in the newsroom after each broadcast, leaning on filing cabinets or on their desks, and reviewing that night's show. It set the tone that responsibility for the programme's success was collective; the team wasn't waiting for Employer Mum or Employer Dad to dish out the praise or the telling-off.

- Consider using apps, which are emerging as another way of giving feedback. We're familiar with 'liking' posts on Facebook, so some companies are enabling their staff to give their colleagues a pat on the back through tapping on their phones. This is a great way of dismantling the highly structured, HR-owned world of appraisals by implementing something that could work for your people.

The irony is that when you stop doing annual appraisals it feels like you're doing less, but in fact you're doing so much more that's of value. And the feedback from organizations starting to put these new techniques into practice is incredibly positive. Accenture, for instance, has moved away from ratings. When I talked to one of its senior leaders about this, she said the conversations around performance were now completely different from before. She felt more relaxed during the meeting because she didn't have to give out a number at the end, which meant she was able to have an engaging conversation about performance. In fact, Dr David Rock has just produced some research into 33 companies that have moved away from ratings, and all of the feedback is extremely positive.[6]

So how can we manage performance in a more effective way?

The don'ts

- Don't do it annually. You can't go with the ebb and flow of your business once a year; it's an artificial construct.
- Don't set individual objectives; set team objectives instead.

- Don't grade or rate; it's dehumanizing and stressful.
- Don't do forced rank distribution.
- Don't do company-wide 360 reviews.

The dos

- Think about how you can appraise teams rather than individuals.
- Give continuous, context-based feedback.
- Accept that performance management is a part of everyday working life.
- Make it easy for your managers to give feedback by affording them a range of personalized options.

Let's finish by looking at how implementing these changes around performance management will help you treat your employees as adults, consumers, and human beings.

Adults

- Giving feedback as equal-to-equal means your staff will feel more comfortable talking about their shortcomings, as well as how their managers could help them more effectively.
- Encouraging staff to seek feedback from their managers enables them to become more pro-active in other areas as well.

Consumers

- Being given feedback informally and on the job means staff are more likely to change their behaviour for the better.

- Having a range of feedback mechanisms means your people are more likely to engage with what they hear.

Human beings

- Not categorizing your employees by rating means they will feel more motivated.

- Moving away from an annual system takes account of everyone's need for more regular feedback.

- Setting team objectives encourages closer team working.

10

Reward

The Easter break was a welcome one for Dave. It came at the end of an incredibly busy quarter. With the whole office putting in extra hours to exceed their sales targets for the financial year, it had been a tough period, and as he drove into work on the Tuesday he couldn't help but feel a little resentful of the toll this frantic patch had taken on his personal life. Walking in the door to his office he noticed something odd about the atmosphere. Everyone was smiling and looking – there's no other way to describe it – like kids in a candy store. Catching the mood, he smiled back and strode to his desk, upon which was placed a giant chocolate Easter egg with a handwritten note from the CEO attached. 'Look inside – right now', said his colleague Sarah. With a sense of childish excitement he cracked open the egg and found £100 inside. 'Wow! Have we all got one?' he asked. 'We certainly have', she replied.

This is a true story and one which Dave told me quite recently. It's a lovely tale, but do you know what's most remarkable about it? It happened ten years ago but he still remembers it as if it were yesterday. In fact it went down in the company's history as being the best reward the employees ever received. It was unexpected, it was thoughtful, and it was human.

Recently I chaired a debate on reward with seven people on the panel. I asked them to tell the audience the best reward they'd ever received. Interestingly, all seven named something different: increased autonomy, flexible working hours to help with a new baby, a development opportunity, a personal gift, a personal thank-you note, a recognition award, and a life-changing bonus. Here were seven different people, with seven different sets of needs, and only one person mentioned money. This tells us a lot about what's wrong with how we reward people today.

The problem with how we reward people

As much as we all love our jobs, we wouldn't do them if we weren't paid. So deciding who gets rewarded for what, and by how much, is always a sensitive area of HR's work. In this chapter I'm looking at the main elements of reward together: salaries, bonuses, pay rises, benefits, and gifts.

For most companies pay is their single biggest expense and yet HR makes decisions about it based not on an understanding of the impact it has on employees, but on what's been done in the past and what their leaders have experienced themselves. They also assume it's money that primarily motivates their staff, whereas, as we've seen in previous chapters, there's now an overwhelming body of research that proves this is far from true.

In my view reward is possibly the most entrenched area of HR; after all, changing contractually binding pay arrangements is no simple matter. When we try to alter things we end up tinkering with the different elements, adding the odd tweak to bonus schemes and pay awards here and there instead of looking at it as a whole. As a result we tend to leave the bulk of reward structures intact from year to year with over 90% of companies retaining a traditional reward framework of salary plus bonus plus benefits. And yet the Net Promoter Score average for rewards programmes is minus 15. So no one is really happy with the way rewards operate but no one is doing anything much to change it.

So let's do that now. What do employees really think about how they're rewarded, and does it motivate them to do their best work? We could ask the following questions.

- What role do we want money to play in terms of reward?
- What does our approach to reward say about us?
- How does it represent our culture?
- Does it reward the behaviours that matter most to us as a business?

Even if you work for one of the companies that does manage reward in a more holistic way, taking into account salary, bonuses, pension contributions, and gifts for each employee, you're probably still not thinking about how it affects your staff as individuals. Every person's relationship with money is complex and unique, so why do we think everyone should be rewarded according to a blanket set of rules?

What's more, embedded within our assumptions about reward are two myths.

- Money is a great motivator.
- We have to differentiate one person's performance from another's solely through their reward.

I'll debunk these later in this chapter.

Using reward as a motivator instead of a sledgehammer

You'll remember motivation researcher Dan Pink's book *Drive* from Chapter 5; in it he challenges our assumptions about the role of pay in incentivizing people to perform well. We all know companies typically try to keep base salaries low and incentivize their people through bonuses, but in fact Pink says we should do the opposite. His view, and those of some other companies I'll talk about in a moment, is people should be paid salaries which are both fair and high enough for them to feel motivated in themselves; if an organization doesn't pay someone 'an adequate amount, or if her pay isn't equitable compared with others doing similar work – that person's motivation will crater'. He even says that 'providing an employee with a high level of base pay does more to boost performance and organizational commitment than an attractive bonus structure'. The upshot of all this is that 'the best use of money is to take the issue of money off the table … Effective organizations compensate people in amounts and in ways that allow individuals to mostly forget about compensation and instead focus on the work itself'.[1]

Let's allow that to sink in for a moment. The best use of money in terms of reward is to pay people a salary (not a bonus) that's high enough for them not to think about it as an issue, so they can focus on doing a great job instead; it's 'off the table'. And I have to say I completely agree with this. In all the exit interviews I've done, the primary reason for the employee's leaving was rarely related to pay; it was usually because he didn't get on with his line manager or wasn't getting promoted quickly enough. Pay was always a secondary consideration.

So how does this approach to pay work in real life? Costco, the US retail giant, has for years paid its workers materially above its main competitor, Walmart; according to the SHRM Foundation's *Creating a More Human Workplace Where Employees and Business Thrive*, in 2013 it paid its average worker $20.89 per hour, or around 65% more than Walmart. Over time this has given it a competitive advantage; Costco's employees generate nearly twice the sales of Walmart's, the company has a lower staff turnover, and it's reduced the costs of recruitment and training thereby saving hundreds of millions of dollars a year. It also has the lowest staff theft rate in the industry. Most importantly, between 2003 and 2013 its stock rose more than 200% compared with Walmart's 50%. I'm sure there are reasons for this other than its salary policy but what's telling is how Costco has taken the issue of pay 'off the table', and by doing so has driven much greater levels of motivation and commitment – discretionary effort if you like – without incentives.

Let's also consider the view that intrinsic motivators are more powerful than extrinsic ones like money. Intrinsic motivators include things like the need for autonomy, the desire to do the right thing, the aspiration to be connected to something bigger than ourselves, and the drive to do work that feels significant and meaningful. There's a huge amount more motivation to be found in these than in the traditional carrot-and-stick approach embodied by the annual bonus scheme.

There is evidence to suggest offering a financial incentive can drive *short-term* increases in performance, but there are also significant unintended consequences of this. In her brilliant book *Wilful Blindness*, Margaret Heffernan devotes an entire chapter to the role of money and incentives in organizations that were later found to be engaging in unethical behaviour. She sums it up beautifully thus: 'Companies use financial incentives like a sledgehammer in the delicate china shop of human motivators'.[2]

The huge amount of research done in this area over recent years shows rewarding *individual* behaviour leads to less collaboration, a lack of willingness to help others, a greater level of isolation, and more selfishness. But if we think about the disrupted world we're operating in, what we definitely need more of is collaboration, trust, generosity of spirit, and connection between people. This enables companies to adapt to new business models, embrace change, and work together to survive. And as Heffernan shows, individual performance rewards at their worst can even create a moral hazard for employees; when you look at the bad and unethical decisions made by institutions, their financial incentive structure is never far away.

How this affects our bonus structure

When I talk to HR professionals about remuneration, most are quick to understand the principle that giving someone a rating in his appraisal doesn't motivate him. But they still find it incredibly hard to let go of the notion we should give people a bonus based on that number. Going back to the previous chapter, we can see how the way we manage performance could be so much more effective if we didn't feel the need to use it for the allocation of bonuses. It goes without saying that rewarding someone with a financial sum is somewhat dehumanizing, and it's not necessarily the money an employee is striving for in any case.

What's more, the mechanisms we have to calculate bonuses are complex. You know the drill: x% based on group results, x% on team results, and x% on individual objectives. Throw in an earnings hurdle and a few other variables, and we have a sum that's incomprehensible for most people. Sometimes the amount of money is actually very low, but it still causes endless amounts of frustration for all involved. I can safely say I've never worked anywhere in which the bonus scheme didn't cause far more problems than it solved; it was always demotivating, complicated, and time-consuming.

It gets even worse when a sense of entitlement is attached to it. One company I'm consulting with at the moment has traditionally given out large bonuses, but its employees are so used to receiving them they take them for granted. Where's the motivation in that?

At this point you may be wondering why, if pay and bonuses are so ineffective at motivating people, those same people will stay at a company that pays them better than the alternatives (as per my Costco versus Walmart example) or do unethical things to achieve a bonus. The answer lies in the overall package. When employees are amply rewarded in their regular pay and aren't incentivized through bonuses, they find more constructive ways to motivate themselves to do a good job. But when they're driven purely by financial targets, they'll focus on achieving those to the exclusion of everything else because they see the size of their bonus as a reflection of their worth.

So there's a lot of evidence to suggest bonuses drive the wrong behaviours, are complicated, are seen as an entitlement, and frustrate people. They certainly don't motivate anyone to excel. What can we do instead? This is new territory, but many forward-thinking companies are experimenting with new options which I'll share with you.

Better ways to give rewards

As we've seen, rewarding individuals for personal achievements is divisive and can create a toxic culture of non-collaboration. US social media company TINT got rid of sales commissions when it recognized the sales process is actually a complex one involving many different employees in the customer life cycle. Marketers, account managers, IT developers, ongoing customer support staff – all have a role to play. It felt paying sales people differently to the rest of the organization was divisive, and it wanted to weed out selfish behaviour and encourage true collaboration. Its solution was to replace individual commissions with a monthly team bonus to reward everyone who 'touched' the customer, related to their role in the process.[3]

Reward consultancy NextJump runs a monthly top ten award scheme. Instead of recognizing individual excellence through top-down nominations it asks its employees to nominate their peers. In these awards only one question is asked: who most helped you to succeed this month? It's got nothing to do with how much revenue that person generated but recognizes the right kind of behaviours instead. HubSpot does something similar and has quarterly peer bonuses where it gives a $100 bonus to anyone who it thinks embodies the company's values.

On the subject of rewarding the activity you want to encourage, you can reinforce the kind of culture you want as well. Accounting software firm Intuit has a special award for the best project failure; it even holds failure parties to celebrate. Its founder, Scott Cook, says every failure teaches us something important and can be a seed for the next great idea; he's worked out that what matters to Intuit as an innovative company is that people shouldn't feel afraid to fail. In a disrupted world every company could take inspiration from this.

Thinking back to my EACH model in which I encourage you to move away from treating employees like children, peer-to-peer reward programmes can work incredibly well. Online retailer Zappos runs one of these in order to foster genuine team spirit. Every employee can grant one co-worker a $50 bonus per month for acts like helping another team member out or wowing a customer. This is far removed from the parental way of delivering rewards, in which senior managers decide who deserves recognition.

So we can see individual financial incentives aren't necessarily the great motivators we believe them to be. Of course, they can have a short-term impact, but we need to be careful about which behaviours we're encouraging.

Motivating teams rather than individuals avoids creating a toxic culture, but if we are going to reward individuals let's do it in a way that encourages collaboration and generosity of spirit.

Is it fair?

Although we in HR spend a lot of time working out reward levels, the big issue for employees isn't so much how they get rewarded as whether they feel it's fair. When I was at the BBC, our pay ratio from top to median was 16:1 and at commercial broadcasters such as Disney or Fox it's 200+:1.[4] Even though we didn't have a highly differentiated ratio we decided to publish the salaries of our top 100 people as part of an exercise on pay transparency, and the response was fascinating. Various senior employees who had previously had no issue with their level of reward became resentful overnight because they discovered their colleague down the corridor was earning £10,000 more than they were. Remember how Dr David Rock's SCARF model shows us lack of fairness is perceived as a threat by our brains? We're unable to feel creative, inspired, or motivated if we're feeling resentful.

Websites such as www.payscale.com and www.paycompare.org.uk make it relatively easy for people to work out what they're being paid in comparison to others, and in many parts of the world there's a growing movement against organizations paying their CEOs and directors vastly more than the rest of their staff. Fund managers and investors are increasingly voting against exorbitant pay deals for directors. Fairness in pay is no longer a personal matter; it's a topic of debate all over the world.

Primatologist Frans de Waal explains this phenomenon using an experiment in which he shows how even animals reject unfairness. In this, two monkeys are trained to use stones as currency; they receive pieces of cucumber in exchange for stones. One monkey, however, receives a grape instead (a superior treat). On witnessing this the other monkey immediately becomes dissatisfied with his cucumber, and actually throws it at the keeper in what de Waal calls a simian version of a Wall Street protest. The clip on YouTube is well worth watching even if only for the entertainment value.[5] It's a brilliant example of how our response to pay and reward is not absolute but comparative.

In HR, however, we focus on affordability (which to be fair is a key issue), and on how to differentiate between people using money. We pay for performance through salaries and bonuses, but what we're actually doing is demotivating people through unfairness. Society is telling us it doesn't like this approach, but that's not informing what we do.

Thanking and recognition

Now we come to rewards other than annual bonuses and salaries.

As we've seen when looking at managing performance, if we want to change behaviour we need to give feedback at the point at which the behaviour is evidenced. In other words, if you see someone doing something great, tell him or her immediately. It's the same with reward. Giving somebody recognition at the end of the year doesn't reinforce the good behaviours because it's so detached from when and where they happened. Some companies are now delivering spot rewards which involve giving an employee a gift there and then; it can be money, a voucher, or even time off. At the BBC we introduced spot rewards and they were a significant success; it was their unexpectedness that was part of their power as there was no sense of entitlement attached to them. Plus they reinforced the great performance at the time when it was shown.

Low-cost can be high-impact

Psychologists and researchers have long been fascinated by the effects of praise on workplace performance and behaviour. In 2004 Gallup conducted a worldwide research project in which it surveyed more than 4 million employees on praise and recognition. It concluded employees who received regular praise were more productive, more engaged, and more likely to stay with the organization than those who did not. They also received higher satisfaction scores from customers, and enjoyed better health.

Offering praise and recognition costs nothing, but studies indicate it can be as effective as giving employees a financial reward. In 2008, strategy consultancy White Water Strategies found being praised can have the same impact on job satisfaction as being awarded a 1% pay rise. This isn't surprising when you consider the Japanese National Institute for Physiological Sciences investigated the neurological impact of praise, and discovered that being paid a compliment activates the same part of our brain as receiving cash.[6]

Ad agency Omelet has a programme called 60/60 which grants employees two hours every week to spend on something they're passionate about, client-related or not. Through this its staff have worked on everything from sports sites to food blogs. When you provide an outlet for employees' passions they know you also value them as unique individuals; this links to Dan Pink's research on the importance of mastery, meaning, and autonomy in our working lives.

Time off is another great way to reward people. In November 2015 LinkedIn announced it was introducing unlimited holiday as a key gift to all its employees. Because it enables its employees to better meet their personal needs, it works incredibly well.

Google has learned through experience that non-monetary awards motivate people better than cold, hard cash. Historically, Google had always offered big cash rewards for its top performers. But it found that these big payouts tended to cause jealousy and resentment and so brought in an alternative approach with a rewards programme that offered experiences – everything from dinners out to new tech gadgets to trips to Hawaii. Employees said they found the new programme more fun, more memorable, and more thoughtful than the cash awards.

At the lowest cost and least complicated end, rewards can simply involve saying thank you and well done. The impact of this is massive and yet so underutilized. The vice chairman of US data management and storage provider NetApp, Tom Mendoza, wanted to make sure his employees knew how much he appreciated their efforts, so he started a movement called 'Catch Someone Doing Something Right'. Every day he calls between 10 and 20 employees across the company to congratulate them on a job well done, as nominated by their peers and managers.

Each call might take only 30 seconds but its impact lasts much, much longer. 'I've never thought short-term things like free lunches, massages, and all the things companies talk about are really what's important to an employee in the long term ... I think people want to be at a place where they feel respected, appreciated, and the company is trying to do something special', he says.[7]

He's right, isn't he? How often do we get that little phone call or handwritten note that makes us feel like a million dollars? I remember when one of the non-executive members of the BBC board was going through a difficult time with another company he worked for, and as a result had to appear at a Public Accounts Committee. I sent him a quick text on the day telling him I was thinking of him. Imagine my surprise and delight when a few days later a handwritten note arrived from him saying, 'Dear Lucy, I just wanted to thank you for your message. It meant a huge amount to me and really helped me get through the day.' With everything he had going on he'd still found the time to send me this, and I've kept it to this day. We value the human touch so much, but we use it so rarely.

In summary, when we look at the research on what motivates people – what makes them feel good about themselves, their work, their employer, and their line managers, and what encourages them to work harder and go the extra mile – there's nothing which suggests paying individuals an annual bonus based on an obscure formula has a positive effect. In contrast, there's a growing body of evidence which shows valuing people for their contribution and paying them fairly – recognizing that people want to be thanked and have their work valued in a way that shows real thought, and is meaningful and timely – is powerfully motivating.

So how can we reward people without annual, individual bonuses?

I'm sure you've gained some inspiration from the examples I've given in this chapter so this isn't meant to be prescriptive, but here are some starting points.

The don'ts

- Don't pay a low salary and top it up with bonuses in order to incentivize people.
- Don't pay annual bonuses that differentiate between individual performances.
- Don't pay individual bonuses unless you tie them into the cultural behaviours you want to encourage.
- Don't assume the only reward people want is money.

The dos

- Think about how you want your employees to feel when you reward them.
- Make sure your pay structure is fair.
- Think imaginatively about how you can reward your staff.
- Reward people at the time when they're showing the behaviour you want to encourage.
- Personalize your rewards so they mean something to the individual involved.

Let's finish by looking at how implementing these changes around reward will help you treat your employees as adults, consumers, and human beings.

Adults

- Giving rewards on a peer-to-peer basis fosters a sense of equality and co-operation.
- Paying people well and letting them decide how they want to use the money is more motivating than giving them rewards through various prescriptive schemes.

Consumers

- Taking account of individual preferences when you reward people means a lot more to them than a one-size-fits-all approach.
- Making rewards timely and regular incentivizes the right behaviour at the right moment.

Human beings

- Moving away from financial bonuses towards intrinsic motivators makes employees feel valued and respected.
- Thinking small and personal in your reward scheme motivates people more effectively than going down the large and impersonal route.

11

Training and development

When I decided I wanted to learn Spanish I looked into a few different options. There were CDs and DVDs I could buy, or I could sign up at my local adult education college for evening classes. In the end I chose to do it via a free app on my smartphone called Duolingo. It's a fantastic tool, and flexible, so I can learn at my own pace. It uses a mix of methods to keep me learning, from games asking me to match the pairs, to repeating words back, and straightforward translation. Not only does the mobility of it mean I can use it on public transport or between meetings, but it also delivers the learning in bite-sized chunks. Every day I access a five-minute learning section (I set my own daily time limits and goals), and it tracks my progress for me. Apparently I'm now 6% fluent! Plus I can share it with friends so if I want to converse and compete with someone else who's also learning we can give each other encouragement. All in all it's pretty brilliant.

Let's compare this to the training we give to our employees at work. We corral them into a classroom, bombard them with PowerPoint slides, and provide no flexibility for the start and finish time. Pretty much the only luxuries that distinguish it from being at school are the cheap coffee and biscuits which are essential for keeping everyone awake. No account is taken of people's

individual learning styles or of how they absorb information differently according to the context in which they're
taught. Most importantly, we don't make that link between what gets learned on the course and how this will
help the attendees do their jobs better once it's finished.

It's not as if there isn't a wealth of information out
there about how we learn. We know 10% to 20% of us
learn more effectively at night or later in the day, for instance, but our courses all run from nine to five. Not only
that, but we expect people to absorb a huge amount of
new information and then remember it all when they get
back to their desks, despite the fact they didn't have the
chance to put it into practice while they were learning. I
remember getting sent on a course at Harvard Business
School when I was HR director of a law firm – goodness
knows how much it cost them. It was an amazing experience and the standard of tuition was excellent, but what
do I remember from it today? Absolutely nothing.

Research tells us we forget 80% of what we learn in
30 days.[1] The US alone is investing $130 billion every year
in work-based learning, two-thirds of which is useless a
month after the course. It's crazy!

We also know that we learn best if we're exposed to a
range of stimuli, such as sound and visuals. If we're able
to practise it straightaway we're even more likely to remember it; this is called multi-modal perception. And yet
most of our courses are two-dimensional with minimal
opportunity to interact and learn through doing.

Actually, the reason we've been doing it the wrong
way for so long isn't a bad one; it's for cost-effectiveness.
It's relatively cheap to put everyone through the same
training in the same way, regardless of preferred learning style. The problem is it doesn't work – we've sacri-
ficed effectiveness at the altar of efficiency. What's more,
we're letting our employees down in every element of

the EACH model here; we're not treating them as adults, consumers, or human beings.

Just suppose you were at home and needed some DIY information. Would you book yourself on a classroom-based course to learn about it? Of course not. You'd look it up online, ask a friend, read a book, or find a YouTube clip. We humans can be pretty resourceful when we want to be. And yet when we're at work somehow this all goes out of the window and we expect our managers to book us on a training day to learn how to do something new.

How we learn to do our jobs more effectively

Research shows we learn 70% experientially, 20% socially, and 10% formally, meaning 90% of how we grow and develop in our roles has nothing to do with being taught in the classic way. So we become better forklift truck drivers by driving forklifts; we become better receptionists by being receptionists; and we become better lawyers by practising the law. We learn socially too, through our managers, peers, and work colleagues, who help and mentor us, and explain how to do our jobs. This is how we get good at what we do.

So instead of wasting money on classroom courses, or their online equivalent, we'd be much better off getting better at spotting opportunities to learn on the job. If we were to put Sally on a new project, for instance, could we supplement the team she's just left with someone who could benefit from experiencing what she was doing before? Work is always creating ways for us to learn.

We could improve our learning by building in the ability to reflect. One of the best managers I ever had was brilliant at this. As we were going into a meeting he'd pull me to one side and ask me, 'What do you want to get out of this?' which prompted me to think more deeply about what I was trying to achieve. He was always creating opportunities for me to consciously learn about what I was doing, with the result that my performance on the job went up more quickly than it would have done otherwise.

Let's think about how we can help people understand their own learning styles and preferences, and factor that into the way we offer training. Mentoring is also a fantastic tool, especially when it's developed formally. How can we put programmes in place for this, not just in a top-down way but also for peer-to-peer mentoring? HR can do a lot to help mentors understand what's expected of them and how best to go about it; it isn't a natural skill for most people. And finally, it's worth reflecting on how information can be shared more widely so there are genuine opportunities for people to learn from each other across the organization.

Who's doing training and development well?

Here are some examples of organizations doing interesting work around training and development. Instead of spending the vast majority of their time in the 10% area of formal courses, they're focusing on the 70% and 20% – the experiential and social elements.

At Sodexo, a food service company, they've tackled the 20% by creating web-based collaborative learning groups called Expertise in Action. Employees can choose to join them so it's not mandatory (in other words, it's adult-to-adult), and they direct their own learning and development. After the first three months of this programme 85% of staff said they could use the learning they gained when they went back to their jobs; it seems helping each other and using the resourcefulness that already exists within a company works more effectively than spoon-feeding.

Technology company Cisco has done some great work in this field as well. It's developed what it calls My Learning Network, an online education tool for all its employees that's mapped to professional skills and job roles. Instead of being an online version of a classroom course, it incorporates remote labs, simulations, games, video modules, and recordings of events. It also focuses on new managers, so they're talking to people at the point when they're most willing to learn.[2]

Hubspot has created the Learn@hubspot video platform with lots of resources for its staff to watch whenever they want, on any device.

Google uses a fun approach that it calls a Whisper Course. This is a series of emails, each with one simple suggestion, or 'whisper', for a manager to try in their one-on-ones or team meetings.

Recently I met with the head of learning and development at LinkedIn, which is building and curating an online repository for its people to use whenever they need it. The finance director, for example, has recorded a video on how to negotiate a deal, so when any of the staff are about to go into a negotiation they can access this short piece of coaching to help them. Just-in-time learning is remembered and absorbed so much more easily than learning when it suits the training department, because it's put into action right away.

At mobile phone operator T-Mobile (now EE), the company has incorporated gamification into its training. More than 15,000 front-line employees have voluntarily completed a set of interactive tutorials, which has resulted in a 31% improvement on customer satisfaction scores.

You can see the democratization of learning that advances in technology have brought about. It doesn't have to happen when it suits HR but when it's most useful for the employee. And with this ability to access training when we like it comes a shift in mindset in which people are expected to take ownership of their own learning as and when they need it.

HR needs to become the curator and quality assessor of valuable training, rather than the controller of how it's delivered. Ensuring staff know how to use their own resourcefulness and then giving them the ability to learn and train at the time that's right for them, and in the way that suits them best, is crucial if we want a disrupted world-ready workforce.

So how can we train and develop our people in a more effective way?

For HR to become an enabler of effective learning, various changes need to take place. To start you off, here are some don'ts and dos.

The don'ts

- Don't assume because you arranged for 15 people to sit in a classroom and be told things that they'll remember and use these things afterwards.
- Don't force your employees to learn in the same way as each other, and at the same time.

The dos

- Think resources, not courses.
- Ask your people how they'd like to learn, and what times suit them best.
- Tailor how you deliver the training according to the topic and audience.

- Think about how you can use all your people to help each other learn and pass on information rather than expecting it to come from a central source.

Let's finish by looking at how implementing these changes around training and development will help you treat your employees as adults, consumers, and human beings.

Adults

- Expecting your staff to identify and satisfy their own learning needs means you're treating them as grown-ups.
- Allowing them to control their training through the use of online modules involves trusting them to discover what's best for them.

Consumers

- Enabling people to learn in ways they find effective is a great way of acknowledging their individuality.
- Making innovative use of technology creates a more personalized experience for the learner.

Human beings

- Shifting to a just-in-time learning system takes into account our human need to practise what we learn immediately.
- Encouraging collaboration and mentorship between staff makes use of our innate social nature.

12

Talent management

Midway through my stint at the BBC, Jeremy, a manager in one of our news teams, sidled up to me at the coffee machine and asked if I had a moment to talk careers. 'Sure', I answered. 'Let's take a seat over there. We can drink our coffee and chat at the same time.'

We discussed the project he'd just completed and what was coming up for him, and I began to sense a level of anxiety in the air. I was surprised at this as Jeremy was one of our most experienced and trusted people. Soon, however, the reason became clear.

'You see, I'm just not sure what the BBC's got in store for me next', he said.

And there it was. He was worried that now he'd finished one project he wouldn't be given another that would help move him forward. In his mind it was HR's responsibility, not his, to find him his next move; it was like the BBC had a secret vault in which everyone's career plans were mapped out and all he had to do was ask for the key. I found this an interesting perspective, and it's one I'll explore later in this chapter, but first let's consider what's wrong with the way we manage talent today – and why we need to change it.

'Talent management' has a bit of a sexy ring to it, doesn't it? But in reality we in HR still take a pretty old-fashioned approach. We expect our best people to join our company, go on a linear career trajectory until they reach their ceiling, and then retire at around the age of 60 or 65. And yet this isn't how many people see their jobs today. Most of us know a job for life is a fairy tale nowadays, but the language we use around career development (*join* our organization) implies a sense of permanency. If the recession – with one in seven people being made redundant in the UK – has taught us anything, it's that the pace of disruption to our working lives has sped up beyond recognition. What's more, we know from what millennials and other employees tell us that people don't necessarily want a job for life anymore; staying two to three years in one company and then moving on is becoming acceptable and even expected.

Demographic shifts have changed everything

Many of the challenges to the traditional model of joining a company and progressing in a linear way are coming from our extended life expectancy. Lynda Gratton, a professor at the London Business School, is an authority on the future of work and her book with Andrew Scott, *The 100-Year Life*, is a fascinating read. In this she explores how we can make the most of the added years we're blessed with today, and exposes as unsustainable the generally accepted view that we should take on continually more responsible roles as we reach retirement.[1]

For a start, walking away from our desks and into the garden centre 30 years before we're likely to die doesn't appeal to all of us. What will we do with all that time on our hands? Work gives us so much more than money; there's the social aspect, and the purpose and meaning it adds to our lives. Around the corner from me, a

94-year-old woman continues to serve customers full-time in her shop each day. 'What else would I do?' she says. In addition, with final salary scheme closures failing even to make the news now, employees can't afford to retire as early as they used to. Clearly for those people with physically demanding jobs there's a cut-off point after which they can't carry on, but in our knowledge-based economy this is less and less the situation. And in any case, do we really want to lose the amazing repository of talent and experience we've built up in our workforces? There are other demographic shifts to take into account. Changes in employment legislation have encouraged more fathers to be actively involved in child-rearing, so they're increasingly wanting to take career breaks as well. And some of us are finding we're looking after our elderly parents in our spare time; my own mum is 75 and is getting more and more frail, so when I'm working out my schedule for the month I often find myself taking her hospital appointments into account.

How our job opportunities are changing

Did you know our corporate structures have become 25% flatter in the last 25 years?[2] This means traditional, well-defined hierarchies are breaking down, with a matrix structure starting to take their place. With this have come changes in the way people 'work their way up' in organizations; it's more a case of travelling sideways and diagonally across the corporate lattice than climbing the corporate ladder, and being able to dial up and dial down our careers when our lives demand it.

There are also more employment opportunities than there used to be. The growth of start-ups and the increasing trend to set up our own businesses or work freelance have given employees exciting new choices in their work.

This, together with the erosion of loyalty to one company for life, means people aren't viewing the linear, corporate career as their only permanent option any more. Artificial intelligence is also starting to make massive changes to the nature of our jobs. Recently I was at a seminar in which the head of Computer Science at Liverpool University explained how robots will soon be able to replicate some areas of medical diagnosis and legal opinion, so one day we may only go to a professional for help with the most complicated problems. In the US, computer scientist Jerry Kaplan[3] predicts 47% of jobs will be computerized over the next two decades, with an estimated 40 to 75 million jobs replaced by computers or robots.

The notion that a particular role will definitely be around in 20 years' time seems somewhat laughable now, doesn't it? Which means supporting our employees to grow through our organizations in a linear way – in other words, the traditional nature of talent management – must be challenged.

It's Employer Mum and Employer Dad again

It's not only the demographic and technological shifts we're going through that make changes to talent management inevitable, it's also the old-fashioned parent–child relationship that needs to change. In HR we don't trust managers to develop their people effectively because we suspect them of hanging onto the best ones instead of thinking about the overall needs of the business. Also, we assume it's up to us to provide the next step in an employee's journey rather than trusting him to find it for himself.

This approach over the years has led people like Jeremy, who we met at the beginning of this chapter, to hand over responsibility for his career development to HR. And we've reinforced this as:

- Employer Mum, trying to control people's career paths linked to the competency matrices we've drawn up (more about them in a moment); or
- Employer Dad, weeding out the worst performers and helping the business retain the best ones, when we should be expecting managers to do this themselves.

Of course, HR needs to play a role in talent management, but this role should involve enabling adult-to-adult discussions to take place, not taking a blanket approach which compensates for managers who aren't managing their people well.

Let's get rid of the nine-box grid

As you know, the 'performance and potential' methodology of the nine-box grid is usually HR's main tool for managing talent. I won't ask you how many hours you've spent debating with managers and amongst yourselves what language should be used in each of the boxes (is 'low potential' too damning?) and labelling people in an attempt to create a consistent approach. This activity leads us to focus more on the boxes than the needs of the individual; it's a classic one-size-fits-all attitude to managing talent. We take complex human beings, with their unique needs and aspirations, and shoe-horn them into a simple and inflexible grid. Where does that get us?

Nor does this grid enable us to assess potential. As we've already seen in Chapter 9 ('Managing performance'), it's tricky enough to objectively assess *performance*, so how on earth can we reliably work out someone's *potential?* I've spent countless hours doing this in the past, as I'm sure you have, and I've never been convinced I cracked how to get it right. As Marcus Buckingham says, we humans are subject to various biases. There's confirmation bias (in which we ignore evidence that contradicts our preconceived viewpoint), the halo effect (in which our positive view of one attribute causes us to assume competence elsewhere), and the horns effect (the opposite of the halo effect).[4]

Not only is it impossible to predict what someone will be like in the future, but also, her aspirations are likely to change over time. She may be full of ambition in your company now but could decide to set up a business on the side next year. Or she might not be performing very well at the moment, but that's because of management issues you're not aware of.

The grid also polarizes people into high- and low-potential. Usually the 10% to 20% who end up in the top-right box are the lucky recipients of generous bonuses, retention payments, and promotions. The unfortunate 10% to 20% in the bottom-left of the grid become the focus of a 'move them out' campaign. But what about the vast majority of employees? They're ignored, a bit like how voters in safe seats are overlooked by political campaigners at election time. This is a problem because in order to move people through an organization we need everyone to be developing their career journey, not just those at either end of the spectrum.

Having said that, this system isn't entirely without merit when it triggers important conversations; in many situations it can provide the catalyst for managers to explore important options with their staff, and can also help HR look at where the gaps might be at a macro level. However, in my experience, the good managers already know their people and consider their development without being told to. They don't need the boxes – they're just a tool HR uses to cater for those who aren't nurturing their people already.

This leads me to my biggest frustration with the nine-box grid, which is that very rarely will anything *actually happen* as a result of filling it in. Whatever the boxes say, managers still tend to hang on to their own talent and the poorer managers still don't deal with their low performers. We just feel better because we've got everyone boxed up. My favourite example is one guy at the BBC who was seen as high-potential but had been in the same job for 27 years!

Here's the thing: the challenge with talent management isn't to plot people onto a grid, it's to create movement in organizations and ensure we're enabling our employees to do the best work of their lives.

So how can HR best manage talent?

Don't get me wrong, HR definitely needs to play a part in talent management. If our role is ultimately to create value for our companies, then making sure they're able to utilize the best abilities of all their people is obviously front and central to our purpose. But we must stop trying to compensate for poor managers. Instead of forcing compliance with a talent management process, HR's role should be to create an environment in which people know their strengths and honest conversations can be held about their aspirations. To do this we need to provide information about what's available in the way of new job opportunities, and to make sure employees know what the various job titles around the organization actually mean. At the BBC we had 20,000 people with 5,500 job titles; this wasn't because we had 5,500 different types of jobs, but because similar roles had been assigned different titles over the years according to the terminology of the department in question. So a researcher in one area, for instance, might need some help from HR in order to realize he could apply to be a researcher in another area, even though the role was titled 'insight co-ordinator' instead of 'research assistant'.

Another assumption HR can challenge is the concept of a certain number of years' experience being essential for particular roles; in most jobs, transferable capabilities are just as important as technical know-how. We can share the new thinking in this field, helping managers and job applicants make more inspired and informed choices. Another way we can move things forward is by celebrating movement across boundaries within an organization. I'm sure many of us have experienced the raised eyebrows and 'humorous' comments a move to a different discipline has prompted, so if someone does make a transition we have a great opportunity to shout about it and encourage others.

Finally, HR's role in talent management can be with job and organization design. Here's where we can accommodate people's strengths, and consider the roles of teams and the way our companies should be best organized for the future. I was treated like a heretic when I first arrived at the BBC and suggested it might not be a good idea for people to stay in a role for longer than five years; apparently I didn't understand it takes decades to become the best. But we found that employees who stayed in the same job for ten years or more usually did want something new; the problem was they hadn't kept their skills updated and didn't have the breadth of experience demanded by outside organizations, which meant they stayed stuck. I believe we have a duty in HR to help people understand the importance of remaining employable; it's so easy to forget that by sticking around too long, we become less attractive to other companies and also less confident in our ability to get another job.

There's a three-way responsibility in talent management comprised of employees, managers, and the wider organization (in other words, HR). Each party has a role to play in making sure the company gets the people it needs both now and in the future. HR's role in this is to ensure there's enough movement of people to provide fresh air at the top, while at the same time recognizing it's up to individuals to find their own way there.

Talent retention

It goes without saying that both HR and managers want to retain their best people. However, what tends to happen is the poorer managers don't recognize when they've got someone able who wants to be stretched, so after that employee's third unsuccessful internal promotion he'll probably hand in his notice. At this point we in HR go into reaction mode and offer him a pay rise or a retention bonus to encourage him to stay, knowing this is shutting the stable door after the horse has bolted but not really having any other option.

We know it's pointless to throw money at this situation. Any prospective employer can easily buy out the retention bonus, and if that person is actually worth more money then why weren't we paying him appropriately in the first place? Once someone has resigned an emotional bond is broken and money will only work for a short time at best. The reasons the employee wanted to leave in the first place will at some point resurface, and as we've already learned in Chapter 9 ('Managing performance'), they're rarely to do with money in any case. Let's find better ways of retaining and managing our talent.

How HR can do talent management the effective way

Talent management can be a messy, complicated business; the needs of the organization, the manager, and the employee are often in conflict. Trying to balance these needs out, especially when they are in constant flux, isn't an easy task. Luckily there are some interesting companies and people who are lighting the way, and I'll give some examples here.

Reid Hoffman, the founder of LinkedIn, is the author of a brilliant book called *The Alliance*.[5] In it he exposes how the traditional employer–employee relationship is based on a series of dishonest conversations. Companies expect loyalty without committing to providing secure jobs in return, and employees leave as soon as something better comes along. His view is more dispassionate than most, in that he advocates creating a new framework in which both sides can keep the promises they make to each other but in a different way. Instead of seeing employees as their property, companies should view them as 'allies', which leads to a relationship based on how they can add value to each other. And this can be based on a specific time horizon which acknowledges the employee will want to leave at some point. The real task for the company is to build the kind of relationship which convinces great people to stay.

What a refreshingly adult-to-adult conversation it would be if a manager and an employee were able to sit down and have an open discussion in which both sides acknowledged the relationship would probably last a certain number of years and no more. During that time the employee would do her best work and fully commit, but towards the end of, in Hoffman's words, her 'tour of duty', she'd want to have a different kind of conversation. Similarly the employer wouldn't promise a job for life but would feel excited about the prospect of his employee doing wonderful things for him over that period. How much more grown-up this would be than the current scenario of people skulking around pretending to have dentist appointments when their next external job interview comes up.

I'd also like to share with you two interesting innovations from the BBC, one I introduced and one I had nothing to do with (but I wish I had).

Like many organizations a few years ago, we'd flattened our structures considerably, taking out 30% of senior management roles over a three-year period. Although this made us more agile and cost-efficient, the downside was a reduction in promotion opportunities. This was a concern because given the 100-year-life scenario I talked about earlier and the removal of the legal retirement age, we might have people sitting in the top jobs for a long time; this would stifle new talent and fresh ideas coming through. The organization wasn't in growth mode so we knew the only way to create movement was to encourage some people to leave. Now we predicted this would be a difficult task for managers for obvious reasons, but instead of asking them to think about it in terms of people we asked them which *roles* they felt needed to be refreshed in the next two years. This led to our introducing what we called the Five and Five sessions. Managers brought forward the names of five people who were high-potentials and ready for a move, and the five roles they felt needed refreshing. This didn't lead to a huge amount of change, but it did create many honest conversations with the people who were in those positions; what's more, we were able to achieve this without being personally critical of anyone's performance.

The other initiative which was brilliant, and sadly not my idea, was something called Hot Shoes, introduced by the BBC North team in Salford to create a more flexible and fluid organization there. In this initiative the HR team helped organize short-term work experiences in other teams which they advertised in user-friendly places like the lift lobby; someone working in Health and Safety, for instance, could apply for a Hot Shoes placement in BBC Breakfast production. It gave people some insight into other roles around the business and in doing so created awareness, connections, and a sense it was possible to branch out and eventually apply for roles elsewhere in the BBC. Not only was it hugely appreciated by the people who participated in it, it was (and this was crucial) supported by HR and the leadership of BBC North.

HR has a role to play in enabling people to think beyond the traditional, linear career trajectory; we have different needs in our working and personal lives, and these go on changing. Deloitte has done a lot of work in the area of what it calls the 'lattice' organization. It's a systematic approach that looks at the four dimensions of a career: pace, workload, location, and role. In collaboration with their managers, employees can customize their careers by selecting options within each dimension based on their career objectives and life circumstances at the time (within the context of business needs). So a high-flyer who has reached partner level might decide she doesn't want to do that until she's 60 – she may prefer to take a step back and work part-time. There doesn't have to be a stigma attached to moving downwards or sideways, and in fact the four elements help to achieve that because they're simply options rather than representations of values attached to particular outcomes.[6]

SAS, a US software company, does something similar which has helped it achieve a tiny staff turnover rate of 3% compared with the industry average of 20%. It attributes most of this to its lattice-like thinking on talent management, which includes its work/life integration programmes. Instead of having stagnant career ladders, it's constantly re-evaluating the needs of its business compared with the needs of its people, moving employees around the organization and giving them the option to ramp their ambition up or down according to their life stage.[7]

Nestlé has introduced a different approach to talent discussions. Instead of leaders being asked to identify which of their people are ready for a move, they are asked to consider talent management from the position of 'everyone in my team is ready'. The idea behind this is to encourage leaders to think more broadly about the career potential for each of their team, rather than a small elite.

And we're seeing trends around a much more fluid and agile approach to talent discussions such as Western Union's 'Talking Talent' sessions, where clusters of around 10–12 managers get together for just one hour a month to talk about the people in their team and the opportunities they have coming up. This makes so much more sense than a once-a-year talent review. Most leaders like talking about their people. They just hate the prep work and the documenting of their assessments and decisions.

So how can we manage our talent in a more inspirational and hands-off way?

I hope these examples have stimulated some ideas about the alternatives to seeing talent management as a way of moving people up a corporate ladder and controlling their career path. Let's get away from the parent–child approach in which HR sees their role as one of a shepherd guiding a flock upwards through the hierarchy, and focus instead on fostering an environment in which the relationships between the organization, its management, and the individuals within it can play out – each party having a clear picture of the risks, responsibilities, and options available.

Here are some don'ts and dos.

The don'ts

- Don't assume your employees all want to carry on moving up the corporate ladder until they retire.
- Don't assume total responsibility for their career development – it's up to them.
- Don't use talent management as a way of compensating for poor managers who don't develop their staff.
- Don't use the nine-box grid.

The dos

- Create an environment in which people are free to move upwards, sideways, and downwards.
- Try to remove the stigma attached to wanting to stay in a role, or with a company, for a limited period of time.
- Consider the needs of your teams as well as your individuals.
- Encourage your people to learn more about your organization by allowing them to work in other areas on temporary placements.

Let's finish by looking at how implementing these changes around talent management will help you treat your employees as adults, consumers, and human beings.

Adults

- Placing the responsibility on employees to develop their own careers, while at the same time supporting them, encourages them to be proactive.
- Encouraging honesty between employer and employee about the length of time the employee expects to work in a job fosters an atmosphere of respect and integrity.
- Giving your people the information they need about future roles in the company, changing job designs, and the new skills they'll need equips them to make the choices that are right for them.

Consumers

- Recognizing the different needs of employees at various times in their lives, and giving them the stigma-free option to move sideways or downwards, enables them to be treated as individuals.

Human beings

- Stopping retention payments to people who've handed in their notice avoids treating them as objects to be bought and sold.
- Encouraging career conversations shows you value your employees' aspirations and hopes for the future.

13

Leadership development

Leadership is a huge topic; type the word into Google and you get nearly 3 billion results. I'm the first to admit I'm not an expert in this area so I'm not attempting to write the definitive piece on leadership. Instead I'm wanting to explore HR's role as regards our leaders and how we can help to spark new capabilities in the pivotal people we look to for guidance and inspiration.

In the past, leadership was always seen as a command-and-control phenomenon; the leader had all the answers and was considered better, stronger, and more talented than the rest of the team. He typically managed within his own staffing, budget, and responsibility boundaries, and was also the one considered best placed to identify his successors. This stereotype of the forceful, charismatic leader figure is a popular one in our work culture and is proving hard to shift. I remember creating a list of leadership competencies at the request of a previous boss and he said, 'There's one thing missing – it's the X factor.' He was looking for that person who could inspire everyone just by walking into the room, which is of course impossible for most people to achieve. And yet this assumption about what a leader is has led us to worship a set of egocentric leaders who haven't necessarily done us a whole lot of good. In my view the reason there's a disproportionate number of high-ego, sociopathic, narcissistic people in leadership roles is because until now we've put them on a pedestal and treated them as if they're on a different level of humanity. The fascinating book *Snakes in Suits*[1] by Paul Babiak and Robert D. Hare examines the disturbing link between psychopaths and leadership. The authors reckon approximately 1% of the general population are psychopaths but among leaders the figure is 3%.

However, today in our disrupted world we need very different things from our leaders; no longer will we follow someone just because he tells us he's correct. Even before the current crisis, business was transforming so quickly, and new technologies were disrupting the status quo so profoundly, that no leader could be expected to have all the answers. Not only that, but the boundaries leaders have previously worked within are dissolving; for them, expecting to liaise every day with the same team in the same function is unrealistic. Virtual, global, and matrix teams all demand a high level of flexibility, insight, and curiosity from leaders to make them work effectively.

HR's role in leadership so far

So how has HR traditionally influenced the state of leadership in our organizations? There are four main things we do.

- We set standards for leadership.
- We identify future leaders through testing and assessment.
- We try to develop them through training and mentoring.
- We compensate for poor leaders.

Setting leadership standards

Every organization I've worked within has its own leadership competency framework, and I'm sure you've got one too. At the BBC we had a wildly complicated set of behavioural indicators for leaders. They also outlined what they needed to be good at in such comprehensive terms that an alien from outer space would be forgiven for thinking we were breeding some kind of master race.

Not only that, rarely do we set leadership standards from the perspective of how it feels to be led by one of these people; all the focus is on the individual and how brilliant he or she should be. This is where we still get the focus wrong; leaders can only lead teams which are inspired to follow them.

Finding our leaders

So how do we identify our great leaders of the future? In the last chapter we looked at how HR creates a talent pipeline. As we've seen, the nine-box grid may identify who's doing a good job today, but it doesn't necessarily predict who's going to be a great leader tomorrow.

The other way we try to spot who has leadership potential is through psychometric testing. I've always been somewhat cynical about these tests, partly because they're an attempt to package up human nature into neat parcels, but mainly because I've never seen a poor test result change the mind of the recruiter (who has usually made his or her mind up already) or indeed that of the person taking the test. When I was HR director at Serco we spent a fortune on a two-day assessment centre in which our top 100 leaders were processed and analyzed. I happened to do my assessment with Grant, the chief operating officer, a self-assured guy who I was sure would 'outperform' me.

When I got my results I remember feeling worried by one particular low score I'd got, whereas Grant just laughed at his despite the fact they were no better than mine. And did either of us make changes to the way we operated as a result? I think you can guess the answer to that.

Let's take a look at the succession-planning process, in which we ask our leaders who they think would be the best people to follow them. There is an inherent weakness in this tradition, which is that leaders tend to recognize other leaders as those who are 'like them'. This results in their selecting people who have the same command-and-control dynamic as they do.

Having said that, I'm in favour of sourcing leaders from within the organization; in fact, an interesting study by risk management company Willis Towers Watson showed that external hires cost on average 38% more than internal ones, but internal promotion hires led to an average increase in total shareholder return of 16.4% after one year. This shows there's a significant performance benefit to growing your own leaders. But it also noted in order to develop effective leaders, companies must allow them to progress through different roles along non-linear career paths, suggesting the way we go about our succession planning needs serious review.

Leadership training

So we've set our leadership standards, we've assessed our people against them, and now we need to develop the leaders themselves. This is another area in which a vast amount of money is spent: $14 billion annually in the US alone. A top-end business course can cost $150,000 per person. And yet despite the propensity for companies to splash out on training, in 2009 business school Ashridge stated only 7% of managers polled felt their companies managed leadership development effectively. Where does this disconnect come from? There are a number of sources, many of which reflect the issues surrounding training which I highlighted in Chapter 11 ('Training and development').

First of all, our leadership programmes tend to follow a one-size-fits-all model; it's like we process the leaders through a sheep dip. They also tend to promote the notion of the superhero leader, perfect in every way. If you think back to Chapter 9 ('Managing performance') and what Dr David Rock says about humans being able to change only one behaviour at a time, this makes no sense. Leadership programmes often try to change 20 or 30 things at once, which is completely unrealistic.

Training and development programmes also overlook the fact that if we're not good at something there's usually a good reason for it. It's unlikely that someone who's talented at working with people can also become an operational effectiveness guru, so why don't we encourage our leaders' strengths rather than force them to up their game on their weaknesses? If we want inspirational leaders, the last thing we should be doing is encouraging them to become similar to one another.

Also, given we know we retain only 10% of what we learn when we don't get the chance to put it into practice straightaway, how can we justify the classroom basis of virtually all leadership training? It has always amazed me how much companies spend on sending their leaders to top business schools in which they closet themselves away for six weeks. Given they usually already have top degrees, MBAs, and PhDs, another qualification is the last thing they need – it's the practical application of their knowledge they could use some help with.

What do we do with the poor leaders?

So many of HR's processes and policies have been created with the good intent of making our leaders better, but unfortunately this perpetuates the parent–child dynamic so prevalent in our organizations. By not trusting managers to lead well, we've created the rod for our own back that's the plethora of matrices, charts, and structures catering to the behaviour of the lowest common denominator. We kid ourselves into thinking that if leaders are following a procedure, however poorly, and they've had their performance review, they're okay. But we're not addressing the fundamental problem which is that many people struggle to manage and lead their people effectively.

If your child is learning to ride a bike, you can give him stabilizers to help him on his way, but ultimately your ambition is to take them off. And yet what we do with struggling leaders is carry on holding the bike seat while they trundle along, continuing to make them do something they're not good at but not helping them to move off on their own either. We do this because having a series of difficult conversations with under-performing leaders, and training them to be better in a way that works for them, is so much more challenging than creating a new policy for them to follow. Plus we continue to promote highly skilled technical people into leadership roles for which they're ill-equipped.

Leadership development in the future

So what can HR do to nurture the leaders we need as we move into the future? The actions we should take are closely related to what we're doing wrong right now.

Set new leadership standards

It's our responsibility in HR to ensure our organizations understand what good leaders are made of. This is no easy task – after all, we're trying to get old-style leaders to recognize we don't want more leaders like them! But this is vital and I don't think we do enough to communicate that what's worked in the past won't necessarily be right for the future.

As an example of how this can be done better, an airline decided to take an alternative approach to traditional succession-planning. Instead of asking its leaders who they would recommend to succeed them and getting 'more of the same' answers, it questioned its employees on whom they already went to for support, inspiration, and connections. The result was the identification of a pool of potential leaders who had their staff's respect and affection.

Abandon the quest for the superhero leader

Competency matrices create the illusion that fully rounded people actually exist, and of course we know they don't. We need to have honest conversations with our leaders about what they're great at and where their weaknesses are so we can help them build the teams which will make them stronger.

Let's look at how taxi platform Uber has innovated with this. When it takes its brand to a new city it employs a three-pronged leadership model: a general manager, a community manager, and a driver operations manager. It knows one person can't be good at everything – it's far more effective for each to play to his or her individual strengths.

Crucial to this is how HR can help managers and leaders understand themselves more deeply, so they know what they're naturally good at. Google realized if its leaders had more self-knowledge they'd be able to recognize what kind of team members they'd need to compensate for their weaknesses, and would therefore be better able to get the best from their people. In 2007 it developed its first Search Inside Yourself workshop, which thousands of its employees have since attended. The emotional intelligence workshop looks at mindfulness, self-awareness, motivation, empathy, and social skills (or, as Google calls them, 'leadership skills'). You can see how learning more about these areas would help a leader get great results from his or her team.

Focus on the outputs you need

Instead of trying to identify all of the competencies and attributes you want from a leader, why not follow SAP's example and simply identify the outputs you expect? It identified three things a great leader does.

1. They coach their team.
2. They show appreciation.
3. They lead with trust.

By focusing on the outputs that a leader would have they were able to free themselves from overly complex competency frameworks and instead allow the leaders to lead in a way that makes the most sense to them – as long as their team felt appreciated, were helped to perform, and were given the autonomy to do their jobs. This enables you to accommodate the different styles of leadership (introvert versus extrovert, for example) and different team dynamics (virtual versus based in same office, for example) whilst providing a useful framework to measure the performance of your leaders against the outputs you require.

Focus on 'on-the-job' learning

Cisco Systems offers job rotation as part of its leadership development; moving around the company and broadening their experiences teaches its people far more than they would learn on a course. IBM does the same. In its case, rotations last for one year, and at least two of them will be in a location other than an employee's home region. This allows its leaders to learn about their jobs in different operating contexts and places.

General Mills, a US company permanently installed in the 'top places to work' lists, says between 80% and 90% of its managers are in place as a result of internal promotions. According to its CEO Kendall J. Powell, the biggest career derailers 'tend to be deficits in individual leadership qualities like integrity, willingness to listen to advice, and resilience – the things that tell you who the person really is'. In order to identify its future leaders it uses a collaborative evaluation process, talking to people across the organization; it feels this is a great way to ensure people get 'multiple looks'. It understands leaders come in different shapes and sizes, so taking the time to identify them by talking to their direct reports as well as other leaders is essential.[2]

Some companies even swap leaders with other companies as part of their development. When FMCG manufacturer Procter & Gamble wanted to learn more about the Internet it discovered Google also wanted to learn more about consumer packaged goods marketing, so they interchanged some executives for a three-month assignment. What a brilliant and open-minded approach to leadership development; I can only imagine the rich insights each individual gained.

Foster the humanity in leadership

Instead of presenting leaders with a list of skills and capabilities they have to learn, let's help them become amazing human beings. On a basic level, all leaders should be comfortable admitting they don't know all the answers, be able to say sorry if they get something wrong, develop storytelling skills to engage people, and praise their staff in a natural and spontaneous way for doing a good job.

In case you're thinking this is a 'nice to have' rather than essential, you couldn't be more wrong. When the notorious Savile crisis was in full flow at the BBC we did a lot of internal research about staff experiences, both positive and negative. We were trying to discover if bullying and abuse of power still existed in the corporation or whether Jimmy Savile was a one-off. One of the questions we asked employees was, 'Who are the leaders you're most likely to have faith in here? Who motivates, supports, and engages with you?' Around 50 names repeatedly came up. When we asked what these particular leaders did to inspire such trust, the answers were as follows.

- They know my name.
- Their door is always open.
- They ask my opinion.
- They remember what's going on in my life.
- They acknowledge when they've got something wrong.

It's not so hard, is it? And yet HR still isn't helping leaders to communicate in a human way.

So for HR, our role with leadership development is not about teaching effective PowerPoint presentation skills, but about encouraging leaders to have the confidence to share personal stories. It's not about training them in operational effectiveness, but about reminding them to be visible to their teams and available to talk to. And it's not about expecting them to feel invincible, but about reassuring them it's okay to say they don't know all the answers.

We can be role models for this ourselves in HR. I'll admit it's pretty scary to say to your board you're not proposing to spend money on training this year but encouraging people to build up trust and an emotional connection instead, because most of them place a huge amount of faith in the business school leadership courses they themselves went on. But it's brave, and it's only through breaking the mould that we'll we get the leaders we deserve.

So how can we develop the leaders we need?

Identifying and enabling leaders who are future-fit means radically changing the assumptions we make about leadership in general.

Here are some don'ts and dos.

The don'ts

- Don't assume the traditional command-and-control leadership style is the only valid one; there are many different ways to be a great leader.
- Don't send your leaders on classroom-based leadership courses with no practical element.
- Don't ask only your existing leaders whom they would recommend to succeed them.

- Don't create yet another process to deal with poor leaders.

The dos

- See leaders as humans with their own stories and experiences which they should be encouraged to share.
- Find creative ways to spot future leaders by talking to employees at all levels and in all functions.
- Encourage leaders to learn more broadly by moving them into different functions and even different businesses.
- Identify the outputs you want from your leaders.
- Place more importance on 'on-the-job' learning than on classroom-based courses.
- Be prepared to have difficult conversations with poor leaders.

Let's finish by looking at how implementing these changes around leadership development will help you treat your employees as adults, consumers, and human beings.

Adults

- Giving your leaders broader learning experiences means you're placing the responsibility for their development partly in their hands.
- Avoiding policies and processes to compensate for poor leaders means they have to improve their performance.

Consumers

- Reinforcing the strengths your leaders already have, rather than making them learn how to be good at things they're mediocre at, acknowledges their individuality.
- Thinking about the leaders your employees would want to work for, rather than the leaders you assume would be best, means treating your staff as consumers of leadership.

Human beings

- Encouraging your leaders to feel okay about not having all the answers, and to admit their mistakes, will create a more human style of leadership.
- Telling stories and giving their personal opinions freely allow leaders to generate higher levels of trust.

14

Employee engagement and communications

If you could describe the workplace of your dreams, what would it look like? Over the past few years Rob Goffee, emeritus professor of Organizational Behaviour at the London Business School, and Gareth Jones, visiting professor at the IE Business School in Madrid, have been asking hundreds of executives all over the world to do just that. It sounds like a pretty radical project, doesn't it? And yet what they found was surprisingly simple: 'In a nutshell, it's a company where individual differences are nurtured; information is not suppressed or spun; the company adds value to employees, rather than merely extracting it from them; the organization stands for something meaningful; the work itself is intrinsically rewarding; and there are no stupid rules.' What a brilliant summary of the type of company we'd all love to work for, and what an enormously engaged workforce all businesses would have if only they could achieve this.[1]

I'm sure you've heard the word 'engagement' bandied around in management meetings more often than you'd care to remember. If people are 'engaged' it's assumed to be a good thing, like calling a project 'strategic' or 'innovative'. But what does it really mean? My favourite definition of engagement is from Engage for Success, a UK not-for-profit organization: 'the conditions where employees feel motivated to give their best each day, committed to their organization's goals and values, motivated to contribute to organizational success, with an enhanced sense of their own well-being'.[2]

However, despite companies' pouring an estimated $720 million into boosting engagement each year, research organization Gallup tells us engagement levels in the vast majority of our organizations have remained resolutely flat for the past 15 years.[3] This means employees are not feeling any more valued, or like they want to go the extra mile for their companies, than they were at the turn of the millennium. So what's going wrong and who's responsible? To me, there are two groups of people causing this problem: our leaders and HR itself. Let's start with the leaders.

How our leaders are failing to engage their people

Our leaders are an increasingly untrustworthy bunch, aren't they? For a start, they sometimes do bad things. Whether they're at the helm of BHS, the Co-op, Barclays, Google, Starbucks, Volkswagen, BP, News International, or even the BBC, given its failure to control Jimmy Savile, leaders are not covering themselves in glory. Barely a week goes by without some kind of scandal being uncovered over high-level malpractice, disingenuous behaviour, or unethical judgement. No wonder there's a dark cloud of suspicion hanging over our top people. The current crisis has given us a new set of super-villains with the UK's *Financial Times* publishing a rolling list of business 'saints and sinners' chronicling the best and worst behaviours from the corporate world.

There are many who say leaders have always behaved like this, and they're probably right; the difference is that now we get to hear about it. When I was growing up I couldn't have told you who most of our major business leaders were, but these days by scrolling through Twitter, watching the broadcasts of Public Accounts Committees, and reading about them in the paper, I'm starting to feel we're on first-name terms. What used to go on behind closed doors is now played out online and in the press, which means poor leadership and questionable judgements are increasingly entering the public domain.

Another reason leaders are losing our trust is because they're failing to develop a sense of higher purpose within their companies that their employees can connect with. We humans are emotional creatures; I don't think I've ever worked late because I wanted to increase my employer's share price, but I've done so on countless occasions because I was creating something I felt had genuine value. The average CEO, however, doesn't seem to understand this. He feels at ease talking about financial performance, shareholder value, and EBITDA growth, but ask him to explain how his business improves people's lives and he's at a loss. Where's the passion for his company's vision? There are some amazing organizations which do have a big 'Why' and are connecting with it successfully, such as Apple, Unilever, and Lego (more about them later), but they're exceptions rather than the rule.

Linked to this is the sterile, pompous language our leaders insist on using. I mentioned the negative feedback I got about my all-staff emails at the BBC in an earlier chapter, and my critic was right. Just like I did then, our leaders, in a desperate attempt to avoid appearing vulnerable or uncertain, talk and write with all their humanity and humility stripped away. The result is a huge disconnect between them and their employees, because it's impossible to trust someone who communicates like a robot.

For all these reasons the relationship between leaders and staff is not one of engagement and respect, and this is a shame because many of them are doing good work. If only they were able to ignite and inspire their people, they would move mountains.

Why HR isn't helping

The world's expert authors on the topics of engagement and motivation, such as Simon Sinek and Dan Pink, agree employees feel more engaged and motivated if they're connected to a corporate sense of purpose. Being inspired by a higher vision of what we want to achieve, together with having the freedom to get on with our jobs and be trusted to do what we're good at – these things are central for excellent performance. We in HR want to encourage this, but instead of standing back and letting go of the reins we end up instituting a regime of parental control which makes us focus on the wrong things.

There are two main areas to blame.

The values statement

First, we concentrate on getting our company's words right rather than on what would actually help people engage with our organizations. The key output of this is the dreaded organizational value statement. I'm sure you've spent hours in meetings desperately trying to come to some agreement on how to craft your statement: 'Let's change "he" to "they" and "could" to "would" and we'll end up with something that won't offend anyone.' As a result we end up with statements that are bland, meaningless, and ignored by employees, most of whom barely know they exist let alone follow them. The BBC was (and still is) a values-based organization with a strong mission and purpose, and we had our six core values printed on the back of our lanyards. I used to enjoy doing a little test when I ran leadership sessions, asking everyone to recite them without taking a peek. Despite the fact that some of the people present had worked at the Corporation for decades, they could never remember more than one or two.

We also know companies tend to choose similar values to each other, which makes these values pretty boring and meaningless; I analyzed the statements of all the companies in the FTSE 100 and found 'integrity' is a core value in 35 of them, 'respect' in 29, and 'innovation' in 24. We've fallen into using clichés to describe who we are as organizations, and are becoming more and more like clones of each other. It seeps into our promotional material as well; we've all seen those corporate videos in which carefully selected groups of photogenic and ethnically diverse employees are set against stock footage of science labs, technology, global scenery, and charitable activity. If you want to see a brilliant satire of this, check out this hilarious video by Dissolve on YouTube.[4]

Short-term tactics

Second, HR focuses on being tactical rather than on creating sustainable conditions for employees to engage with their leaders. Hands up – how many of you have come up with some wacky way of getting everyone excited about work, like dress-down Fridays or mid-morning singalongs? I know I have (well, maybe not the singalong). These things create a short-term feel-good factor, amongst some employees at least, but can also be seen as patronizing and manipulative. Not only that, they're implemented as one-size-fits-all initiatives, in some cases literally, as one company's issuing staff with 'fun' outsize yellow T-shirts illustrates. Instead, we need to create the conditions in which each of us can tap into our own motivation and inspiration, guided by the overarching purpose of the company.

Another way HR unintentionally waters down engagement is by trying to manage corporate messages far too closely. When the CEO wants to put out a statement about how great our company is to work for, we cascade it down through the organization as a script and a PowerPoint deck. For employees on the receiving end of this communication there is little reason to trust the message. For a start, it doesn't necessarily tally with their own version of reality, and also, the format doesn't allow for any personal interpretation by the leaders who are forced to regurgitate it. And what happens when staff want to debate it, or even disagree with it? There is rarely a channel through which they can do this, nor is it encouraged. So employees are left with stage-managed conferences, all-staff emails, and other forms of top-down communication as their only source of information from their leaders. I remember discovering at the BBC some people had emails from internal comms on auto-delete because they couldn't be bothered to read the same 'on-message' information time and time again.

So what can HR do to improve employee engagement and internal communications?

If our employees are trusted with having the freedom to operate as they see fit (within a framework), if the way we engage with them is tailored to their individual needs, if they're involved in shaping the solutions that affect them, and if leaders behave and speak in a human way by using stories and conversations instead of the tools we set up in HR, then we all stand a good chance of building engagement. We'll be treating employees as adults, consumers, and human beings. Here are some key ways we can put this into practice.

Share the problem, not just the solution

We can build trust by being willing to share not just the solutions we come up with, but also the problems that generated them. At the BBC we were often reluctant to go public with the results of our annual employee engagement survey because we predicted it would reach the media and be used as a stick to beat us with. This was understandable, but then why bother asking staff what they thought in the first place? On another occasion, when a deficit of £1.7 billion in our pension scheme prompted us to devise pension reforms to plug the gap, we knew it would be a massive concern for our people. In an attempt to soften the blow by presenting both the problem and our solution at the same time, we spent ages working out what to tell them. This approach, however, failed to take account of human nature. People needed time to absorb the idea there would be pension changes so they could prepare themselves for when they were announced. It was all too much for them to hear in one go, and this resulted in strikes, anger, and disengagement.

'Start with Why'

As Simon Sinek says in his book *Start With Why*, we all need an overarching purpose in order to feel truly engaged with our work. So instead of devising endless value statements, let's spend the time we would have wasted on them figuring out how to connect our people with a higher goal.

Lego, for instance, talks about inspiring and developing the 'builders of tomorrow' through creative play and learning. If you work for them you're completely clear about what you're there to achieve. Patagonia, the outdoor clothing brand, has a clear mission: 'Build the best product, cause no unnecessary harm, use business to inspire and implement solutions to the environmental crisis.' As they make products for people who are passionate about experiencing nature, this statement shows how their corporate, staff, and customer values are aligned.

Another company which has clearly spent a lot of time thinking about what they're here to do is Whole Foods Market. Here's its higher-purpose statement: 'With great courage, integrity and love – we embrace our responsibility to co-create a world where each of us, our communities and our planet can flourish. All the while, celebrating the sheer love and joy of food.' How emotive and powerful is that? And I can confirm, having emptied my wallet in Whole Foods yesterday, how much its staff behave as if they live and breathe this purpose every day.

But what if your business doesn't save the environment or serve some grand cause? What if it makes widgets or canned vegetables? You could take inspiration from online clothing retailer L.L.Bean. Here's its core values statement: 'Sell good merchandise at a reasonable profit, treat the customers like human beings, and they will always come back for more.' There's no grandiosity about this, no mention of words like 'integrity' or 'innovation', just a commitment to behave well and treat everyone in a human way.

Allow for autonomy

None of us likes to be forced into parroting something we're not comfortable with; it's a bit like having to wear something that doesn't suit us, and it comes across as false in any case. So instead of handing down inflexible messages from on high, we'd be treating our managers with a greater degree of individuality if we let them give their own interpretations of what leaders say. The link between line managers and their teams is absolutely vital, so if you're not empowering them to talk about the 'why' and personalize the message (within a framework), you're not enabling them to put it across in a credible way. Interestingly, one of the upsides of the current crisis is that many of our leaders are having to do without the flash conference and well-rehearsed script to communicate with their teams. I hear regular stories from HR about how the crisis has turned our slightly robotic leaders into more human and empathetic ones, capable of compassion and genuine warmth. They've let down their guard and let their vulnerability show. When they ask the question 'How are you?', they actually want to know the answer, rather than ticking it off their list before diving into task allocation. We see them with their kids, their pets, in real-life environments as they struggle to look professional on Zoom – just like the rest of us.

At Expedia, the leaders have really been encouraged to share their experiences of working from home and say this has helped encourage much more human leadership comms such as a 'senior executive who home-schools five kids who blogged about his experience and has become a wonderful resource for really honest interactions.' The company even has a specific Slack channel that celebrates, through photos, when employees' pets invade their video conferences!

Encourage open discussion

Part of treating employees like adults is allowing them to openly discuss and challenge what's going on in the company. Virgin Media does something it calls 'the Grill', in which senior leaders are filmed being grilled (as the name suggests) by various employees; it's totally unprepared and goes out to everyone in the company. By doing this it's showing it's not afraid of genuine debate, and that it also accepts not everyone will agree with it. If you think about this, it's what everyone in our society is hungering for now. Part of the appeal of reality TV is that it's not stage-managed or rehearsed – it's authentic and real.

Use a range of media to communicate

The most successful consumer advertising campaigns always make full use of a range of media; posters, television, radio, direct mail, and social networks are deployed. This is done to cater to a diversity of preferences, and we can learn a lot from this when it comes to disseminating our corporate information. Usually when HR wants to get across a message they'll do it as a blanket piece; big video messages, conferences, and emails are all favoured methods. Rarely do we take into account the differences in how people interpret information and tailor it to their needs.

Speak like a human

We've all heard the jokes about business jargon such as 'blue-sky thinking' and 'reaching out', but most leadership and internal communications are riddled with it. Every time we use one of these phrases we distance ourselves from our audience rather than connect with them. Just think of the positive impact when someone says 'I'm sorry' instead of 'I apologize', or 'I made a mistake' instead of 'mistakes were made' and you'll understand what I mean.

This links to the use of social media in the workplace. I've already spoken about how we should allow employees to use it within broad guidelines, but it's amazing how many organizations do everything they can to stop it being used. And yet we know people are more likely to trust what their friends or work colleagues say than their leaders, so embracing and encouraging it should be at the heart of every employee engagement strategy. In fact, L'Oréal now reports on Glassdoor feedback quarterly at its board meetings; instead of just doing internal surveys in which it specifies the questions, it's evaluating what its employees are actually saying about it when they're not in the room.

Create a great physical environment

We in HR tend to think of ourselves as separate from facilities management, and indeed these two functions are usually set up as distinct entities. This is a problem, because we know our physical environment is incredibly important to us if we're to feel happy at work. Unfortunately most of us work in one-size-fits-all set-ups in which rows of desks maximize the efficient use of space; the human factor is rarely taken into account in office design. Why not think about how employees use their offices when they engage in various different activities during the day? Introverts may find themselves more productive in a corner office, but for team sessions a livelier space is required.

One of the most exciting new office design trends is a layout which engineers chance encounters between employees; this fosters a sense of community and also, crucially, helps to spark new ideas. Samsung, believing the best ideas never happen when you're sat behind your monitor, has done away with the traditional office layout in its new US headquarters. Instead, vast outdoor areas between floors encourage workers into public spaces.[5]

Of course, the current crisis has led us to question whether any of us will ever be back in the office. As working from home becomes the norm for many, we are having to reevaluate the notion of the workplace. There are some huge upsides, of course – no daily commute, more time with our families, and so on. But we are also Zoomed-out, missing human interaction and lacking the spaces and facilities to be more creative. Surely a hybrid of the traditional workplace and the home-working of the crisis is where we will end up? The crisis has forced us to develop our thinking and practice around the right space for the right kind of work.

Consider the whole person

The crisis has also led us to be more aware of the need to think about our staff as human beings who worry about their kids, health, money problems, and relationships. Many organizations are starting to wake up to the fact that they need to see their employees as 'whole people', and are going further than just providing telephone helplines for personal problems. This can be through line managers becoming more sensitive to concerns they may have shied away from before, such as mental health issues; in fact Unilever[6] has created a mental health programme incorporating manager training and awareness, and also assistance for individuals to improve their own mental health.

So how can we foster a deeper sense of engagement in our employees?

As you can see, HR can do a huge amount to create the conditions for amazing employee engagement and communications simply by changing the way we think about and implement them.

Here are some don'ts and dos.

The don'ts

- Don't create trite, meaningless value statements which you then expect your employees to adopt.
- Don't communicate in 'corporate speak'.
- Don't try to stifle discussion and dissent.

The dos

- Establish a vision for your organization's higher purpose, and find ways of enabling your employees to connect with it.
- Get clear on how your stated culture and values actually work. Netflix's SlideShare document is so unusual because it discards the standard approach. It has nine values, but Netflix's effort went into what they looked like in reality and not simply the company image these values created.
- Encourage your leaders to expose their humanity in their communications.
- Allow leaders and managers to communicate company messages in their own way.
- Enable employees to use social media freely within broad guidelines.
- Find ways of making your physical working environment an enabler of productive work.

Let's finish by looking at how implementing these changes around employee engagement and communications will help you treat your employees as adults, consumers, and human beings.

Adults

- Allowing staff to communicate responsibly on social media makes them feel respected.
- Setting up forums for employees to discuss and disagree with corporate policy treats them as if they have something valuable to say.
- Encouraging leaders and managers to personalize their company messages shows a level of trust towards them.

Consumers

- Spending time getting to know your employees' values and interests, and how they can be connected to the organization's, involves treating your people as individuals.
- Offering your people a more customized employment experience in terms of workspace and communications will help them feel more motivated.

Human beings

- Avoiding bland values statements acknowledges the individual humanity in the organization.
- Enabling leaders to communicate in non-'corporate speak' means they can communicate human-to-human.
- Creating for the organization a sense of purpose that employees can connect to inspires passion and commitment.

Part IV

Making it happen

So every part of HR is in need of a radical overhaul. This feels somewhat daunting and yet the possibilities are incredibly exciting. We've got nothing short of a revolution on our hands.

How on earth do we go about changing HR for the better, given the task is so enormous? The next two chapters are designed to help you with this. Chapter 15 guides you through the practical implementation of your ideas, and Chapter 16 helps you envisage the HR team of the future.

Clearly, how we change HR is a massive topic and the following chapters will address just some of the issues. My follow-up to this book, *The HR Change Toolkit*, provides a lot more detail and gives you the complete step-by-step guide to doing it well.

Turning old HR into new HR

I'd thought it was going to be a happy day – we were finally getting rid of performance ratings from our annual appraisal scheme at the BBC. As I walked into my internal staff meeting with a spring in my step, I found myself surprised at how excited I was to announce this to my team.

I'd love to say the idea for removing the ratings had been due to my revolutionary vision and insight into how pointless they were, but I'd be lying; my thinking on these matters wasn't yet fully formed. The initiative had actually been generated by the unions, who were against them because they saw ratings as a precursor to performance-related pay. They'd even threatened to ballot for industrial action if we didn't eliminate them from the system. However, despite the fact that getting rid of them was purely a pragmatic solution on my part, I did feel excited by the idea as even at that stage I could see they didn't achieve anything.

To my delight the change went through without a hitch. Management were positive about it, as were staff, and, of course, the unions. But when I called a meeting with my internal HR team to discuss how we were going to implement it, many of them were horrified. 'How will we measure people objectively?' they asked. 'How will we know managers are having performance conversations

with their staff now?' This surprised me because I'd assumed they were with me on this, and that they understood appraisals should be about the conversation and
not the grade.

Looking back on this experience, it occurs to me
it exemplifies many of the barriers we face in making
changes in HR today. Some of the hurdles arise because
board members and executive teams are reluctant to face
reality, but many of them come from within ourselves and
our own teams. So let's kick off this chapter on the 'how'
of the HR revolution by looking at why it can be hard to
effect change. If we're not prepared for the difficulties
we'll face, and if we don't understand the reasons why
other people will find it hard to come along with us, we
won't be equipped to meet the challenge head-on.

There are two places you'll find barriers springing
up: in your leadership and in your HR department. We'll
look at each in turn.

Barriers to change originating in your leadership

There are a number of reasons leaders find it hard to
accept changes in HR, but they boil down to three main
ones:

- their ingrained assumptions about what consti-
  tutes good HR practice, and their lack of interest
  in or understanding of the 'people agenda';
- the pressure from external regulators; and
- their preference for dealing with numbers and
  processes rather than people.

At the top of our organizations sit leaders who have
extremely deep-seated beliefs about what motivates people to do a good job. These directors and executives

moved up through their businesses in the 1980s and 1990s and are therefore a product of that age, so let's cast our minds back to what companies were like during that period. Those years saw the growth of the training and development function, the proliferation of executive leadership programmes, the expansion of the annual employee engagement survey, the implementation of forced rank distribution, and the growing use and complexity of bonus schemes. Then in the late 1990s and into the new millennium came an increased awareness of the importance of people in organizations; directors began to realize it wasn't enough to have a brilliant business strategy and that they needed to develop their employees as well. Unfortunately this only went as far as seeing staff as assets, so boards developed tick-box mechanisms such as the balanced score card, which recorded factors such as the percentage of employees who'd had a performance review.

As a result these leaders have been graded and rated to within an inch of their lives, and are used to doing this to other people, too. Their mental HR model is one of seeing employees in numerical terms, so unsurprisingly they have a highly process-driven approach to managing them; if they're no good get rid of them, and if they are then pay them a load of money to stay. And because they're measuring their staff through tracking their participation in courses, appraisals, and surveys, they feel they're already 'doing' people. This doesn't mean, of course, they understand how human beings are motivated to do their best work.

They don't think this way because they're stupid or uncaring – far from it. I was one of them myself until relatively recently. They've just never been presented with a convincing reason to change their view. For this reason when I consult with HR teams across the globe, helping them to transform the way they do things, one of the biggest barriers is the belief that their own leaders won't 'get it'. 'I'm with you on this, but my leaders would never hear of it', they say.

From this you can see that despite CEOs publicly claiming their people are important to them, in reality they're more interested in numbers and operations. They tend to come from finance or operations backgrounds; in fact less than 5% of chief executives have an HR pedigree. From my experience of being an HR director in three different businesses I can confidently say that not once have people issues ever been the number-one item on a board meeting agenda, and I can count on one hand the number of times a chief executive has called me up for an in-depth discussion about people and strategies.

Added to this is the pressure from external regulators who see statistics on how many people have had an appraisal, or have been through training courses, as being reliable indicators of the competence of a company's HR function. I have many clients who are desperate to be more innovative and responsive to how human beings function, but their regulatory bodies still insist that they produce job descriptions, organization charts, and all the paraphernalia of old-school HR management. A bank executive emailed me the other day saying he would love to get rid of appraisal ratings but knew his regulator would resist it. Now I could suggest he try a bit harder to convince them otherwise, but I do understand his predicament.

As you can see, there is a lot of work to do when it comes to convincing leadership of the need for change in the first place, let alone tackling what those changes should be.

Barriers to change originating in HR

We too can find it hard to envisage how things could be done differently, and here are the main reasons why:

- the pressure we're under to justify HR financially in our organizations;
- the ease of staying as we are versus the difficulties associated with change;
- the challenge of proving ahead of time that change will be beneficial; and
- the difficulty of unpicking processes which are interdependent upon each other.

Unfortunately we've been complicit in the entrenched view our leaders have of HR. Instead of seizing the opportunity to be seen as the 'human being experts' in an organization, we've been wanting to prove our worth by showing how our work is increasing the value of our 'assets' – much like finance, operations, and marketing have to do. It's so much easier to produce a new process than it is to change how people operate. It's so much simpler to implement a new organizational structure than it is to improve people's performance. And it's so much quicker to tick boxes than it is to delve into the messy reality of people's minds and emotions. What's more, many HR people started their careers in the policy and processes area of the discipline, which makes it even harder for them to agitate for change. It's no wonder we've made this rod for our own back.

No one in HR is penalized for keeping things safely as they are, are they? We must be one of the only departments that isn't expected to innovate. It feels like it's asking for trouble if we put our heads above the parapet to ask for a change no one wants. Why be brave when we could have an easy life? This is reinforced by the fact we know board directors would like to see evidence other businesses have succeeded in what we're trying to do, so they feel safer in authorizing a change. Ironically, if we were the ones developing the products and services our business's customers pay for, we'd want to be the first to market with our ideas and innovations so we could differentiate ourselves from the competition. But in HR we only seem to want to do something different if our competitors have done it first.

Added to this, the effect of any HR change is usually long-term with the results difficult to quantify. It's taken a heck of a long time for us to get to where we are now, so it stands to reason it's going to be a long haul out of it. When I'm advising HR clients on how to make changes, I encourage them to keep the faith and see it as a long-term project; there's so much emotional and financial investment in the status quo that it will take a lot of work to shift opinions. Going back to the trouble my HR team at the BBC had with accepting the removal of the ratings system, this was partly due to their assumption that ratings were essential, but also to the threat it posed to their policing role. Being hall monitor gave us a certain amount of status, after all.

Another barrier to change is that HR processes aren't usually a stand-alone affair; they're heavily integrated with others. Performance management, for instance, is closely linked with reward, career development, training, and talent management. How do you transform one area without causing a complicated domino effect in the others?

So how do we create change?

Looking at all these barriers you're probably wondering how anything in HR changes at all. So what unites the organizations that *have* begun to turn accepted HR wisdom on its head? What makes them different from the majority? There are two main factors.

- They've made an extremely clear case for change.
- They've matched the changes they've implemented with the needs of the business.

Building your case for change

The companies which have innovated successfully in the HR space have all made a crystal clear case for change. This is why much of the new thinking has recently come from Silicon Valley companies, which have two characteristics that make them different from the rest of us and that make their case for change more obvious. The first is that for them, the war for talent didn't let up during the recession; in fact, it got worse. They weren't just competing for employees with other tech outfits but also with companies like banks and retailers, which required digital experts. This meant they had to think differently in order to attract the best people. The second characteristic is that they've always had a higher proportion of millennials working for them – people who've demanded new and different ways of working. They want higher levels of autonomy and flexibility and have a greater need for purpose in their work. In contrast, those of us in other sectors have often had to artificially create the need for change.

Until the crisis.

For all of the challenges and difficulties of the current crisis, it presents HR with the biggest opportunity for a case for change that we have ever had. If your leaders aren't questioning the need to do things differently in HR, then maybe it's time to polish your CV?!

So how to build the case for change in more detail. First of all, it's worth playing the accountants at their own game and spending time collating both quantitative and qualitative research data to make your case. Remember, you're going to be trying to convince people steeped in financial and operational assumptions that what you're proposing is worth taking a chance on. You might be thinking, 'Hang on, you've just spent most of this book telling me people, with all their contradictions and individuality, can't be bean counted and put into boxes. Now you're saying I should do just that?' Not exactly. You need to be clear on your numbers so you can convince the people who base their decisions on them (and let's face it, numbers do have their place) to trust your case for change. Once you've done that, you can start transforming things for the better.

What kind of data can you use? Performance management is a good example because it's pretty easy to work out what your annual appraisal system is costing you. Here's a process to help you.

1. Work out how long each performance review takes a manager, including gathering feedback, preparing the documents, holding the discussion, and writing it up. Let's assume it's three hours for a review.

2. Take the average manager's earnings per hour including benefits, and multiply it by the number of hours per review. Let's assume the earnings are £100 per hour; this would total £300 per review.

3. Do the same but for the average employee, who will be earning less than her manager but probably spending as long on her appraisal (preparing a list of her achievements, documenting her goals, and having the discussion with her manager).

Let's assume she earns £60 per hour including benefits, which would total £180 per review.

4. Multiply the cost per review for both managers and employees by the totals for each group in your organization and you'll quickly come up with some significant numbers. A company with 700 managers and 5,000 employees would be spending £1.1 million on appraisals every year. This doesn't even cover the IT maintenance costs associated with the online appraisal system, the time HR spends in orchestrating and policing the process, and the hours spent in calibration meetings.

5. Combine this with the qualitative data we already have on how appraisals are valued in terms of improving performance; Deloitte found that only 10% of organizations believe they're worth the time and effort that go into them.[1]

This at least gets you to a place where you can legitimately ask questions. It might not give you all the answers, but it does begin to help you build your case for change. If your company was spending over £1 million on machinery each year it would want to know if it was worth it, so why wouldn't you want to do the same with HR processes?

Another option would be to analyze the effectiveness of your training and development. As you discovered in Chapter 11 ('Training and development') we learn most effectively on the job but spend vast amounts on formal training. We also know 80% of learning is forgotten in 30 days, which means occasional courses are no good. It therefore wouldn't be unreasonable for you to question whether your current training set-up is a responsible use of your company's resources. In no organization I've ever worked in has anyone done this kind of analysis, which means you'll be a pioneer.

Moving on to the qualitative data, this is an area we should pay more attention to. I've never come across a manager who thinks performance reviews are a productive way of spending time, so it shouldn't be difficult for you to build a case for change using personal feedback. How about getting together a group of high-performing people in your company (they could be millennials or a mixed group) and asking for their honest opinions on the processes you oversee? Do they enable them to do their jobs more effectively and improve their motivation and productivity?

When I work with clients on HR transformation I always spend a lot of time helping them build their case for change, because unless you have solid evidence that what you have isn't working, you'll find it incredibly difficult to persuade anyone to let you try new approaches. It really is worth putting a significant amount of effort into this stage.

Matching change to organizational need

Board directors rarely respond enthusiastically to projects which seem to come out of thin air. You'll find it much easier to get support for your initiatives if you link what you're wanting to change to the main problems your business has got, and where there's the highest level of discontent. If you're on a mission to improve your performance reviews, for instance, what is the business problem you're trying to solve?

You should have a good idea about what your board sees as the main issues within your company, but if you're not sure consider this: every organization is after two things – more productivity and more innovation. Your job is to ask yourself, and to demonstrate, how what you're proposing to change is going to help with those two aims; it's only by doing this you'll demonstrate credibility. For example, if you identify enhanced collaboration as the key to increasing both innovation and productivity, you'll have a strong rationale for proposing changes such as job rotation and the setting of team objectives.

Making it work

In this next stage, pick one thing you want to change: perhaps performance management, career development, or employee engagement. Although remember, when we want to change or improve things in HR we have a habit of leaping into the mechanics of the situation and creating a new process or policy rather than taking a step back to examine the principles of what's currently wrong. This is where treating employees as adults, consumers, and human beings comes into its own, because it will encourage you to move away from the 'fix it' approach and reflect on the beliefs and values underpinning what you plan to do.

Treat your employees as adults, consumers, and human beings

In terms of treating your employees as adults, for instance, where is your organization now? Does it trust its people or does it assume there's a need to protect itself from the lowest common denominator? You need to explore these issues in full with your leaders because if you don't do this first, all the unsaid and ingrained beliefs they have around employees and managers will impact their response to any change you propose. Let's say you want to suggest removing a swath of policies which restrict and frustrate your staff. If you try to sell this to a group of leaders who have a fundamental mistrust of their employees, you'll not succeed. You have to start with the underpinning beliefs.

In terms of treating your employees as consumers, it's worth exploring the assumptions of the people you're attempting to convince before you go any further. If their starting point is that all HR procedures must be scalable, monitored, and cost-effective, they're going to struggle with the notion of a more tailored approach. They may 'get it' in their personal lives, but they'll still find it hard to come to terms with in the office. Again, your job is to help them make that connection between the two so they can see the one-size-fits-all process doesn't work. If you don't do this you'll end up simply substituting one process with another and miss the point: that you're trying to cater for a range of human personalities.

And finally, in terms of treating your employees as human beings, explore your leaders' assumptions about what motivates their people. If they're convinced it's all about money, or about giving bonuses and promotions to the best people and not worrying about the rest, then any changes you propose around reward, performance management, and talent management are not going to be well received.

Be realistic

Having done your groundwork by gathering the data, relating your proposed change to your organization's biggest need, and exploring your leaders' pre-existing assumptions, you're well placed for a reality check. This isn't the time to shy away from having a grand vision, but you need to be realistic about how long it's going to take. If your company is hugely parental in its culture, for instance, your best plan might be to adopt a slow but steady approach that would take you many years to complete.

As an example, in the Natural History unit of the BBC we instituted an experiment in which we allowed staff to take as much or as little holiday as they liked as long as they got their work done. This initiative actually came from the department itself, which had a well-motivated and relatively small team, an open-minded leader, and staff who didn't work on complicated rosters. I would never have attempted this in a less suitable department or tried to implement it across the whole organization in one go, but in this one area it worked incredibly well.

Please don't try to change everything at once. Instead, concentrate your efforts on a willing control group and explore different options. Accenture, for instance, have spent a couple of years changing their approach to performance management, with various groups piloting different approaches; by involving the end users, they're ensuring whatever they eventually implement has been thoroughly tested. In contrast, an organization at one of my workshops on performance management called me up afterwards to tell me it'd ditched its appraisal system overnight, affecting 10,000 employees! That filled me with dread, because if there turned out to be any problems with it the organization would be under pressure to return to the status quo immediately. Ensuring you have a realistic sense of your starting point doesn't mean you have to limit your goals – it just means you need more time and support to get you to where you want to be.

Build in regular sense checks

When I talk with HR managers it never ceases to amaze me how readily they leap from acknowledging the redundancy of a process to asking what the replacement should be. I tell them they're missing the point. The next step shouldn't be yet another procedure – it should be devising a way of working that helps and motivates people. For this reason it's a good idea to build regular sense checks into your plans. Ask yourselves if you're slipping into 'process land' because you're not sure if you trust your people to get it right on their own. To help you with this I encourage you (and your teams) to answer the following questions as honestly as you can. You can do this in private or as a group.

- Do I take a parental approach to my employees, either as a caring support figure or as a rule-setter and judge?
- Do I prefer to treat my employees as similar to each other, or do I feel excited by the idea of seeing them as individuals?
- Am I ready to redesign what I do to suit human nature, or do I see human nature as the thing I'd like to change?

Checking in regularly with yourself, and encouraging your team to do the same, will ensure old habits don't derail the innovation and freshness of your original plans.

Focus on the capabilities you have available

The reason we developed so many rules and procedures in the first place was to cater for managers who weren't doing a good enough job on their own. We did this because we passionately believed that supporting people with their careers through the annual appraisal process, for instance, was correct. Now we need to refocus our energies on raising the capabilities of the people we've not been trusting for so long. Of course we know this only works if we have the right managers, and we've spent a lifetime recruiting many of the wrong ones. This means we've got a massive task ahead of us to improve management capabilities, so that when we're finally able to remove the processes, they're ready to adjust.

Quick recap

Here's what you can do to start transforming HR in your organization.

- Build your case for change using quantitative and qualitative data.

- Ensure you're addressing your organization's main business problem.

- Explore the EACH model with your leaders to get them on board with the thinking behind your plans.

- Be realistic with scope and scale, but also aspirational.

- Pilot your changes with end users.

- Build in regular sense checks.

- Focus on building the capabilities of your leaders.

Where does this leave HR now, you may be wondering? What will an HR department look like in the future, and how will this affect your own role? It's going to be an exciting ride – one which I'll explore in the next, and final, chapter.

16

The HR team of the future

'So from what you're saying, Lucy, if we in HR don't turn conventional HR wisdom on its head pretty quickly we'll become extinct. Is that right?' An interesting bunch of HR directors in Madrid posed this question to me, and I'm afraid my answer was a resounding yes. I can foresee chief executives of major companies shedding their HR functions, transferring the compliance and policy elements to their legal and finance teams, and outsourcing the transactional processing to a self-service model. Because where's the inherent value in operational processing and compliance? Our CEOs want our employees to be able to cope in a disrupted world, but that will only come through HR's ability to understand how human beings behave and are motivated. In today's knowledge economy, in which 70% of our assets are intangible, it's all about the people. And unfortunately HR hasn't really been about the people but about operational efficiency.

But I don't want to be negative because I truly believe this is HR's time. This is the moment we can address this issue and make ourselves one of the most relevant and valued teams in any organization – if we're prepared to take action. If HR didn't already exist would we create it afresh? I think we would, but in an entirely new way.

The six trends to follow in HR organizational design

I often get asked what an organization chart of the HR department of the future could look like. Clearly, describing a structure that would work for any company would be meaningless, so instead I'll go through six key trends in HR design that will increase your employees' creativity, innovation, and productivity. Happily, they should save you money as well.

Here are the trends in summary:

- moving away from HR business partners in favour of HR account managers;
- creating a self-serve HR advisory function which is a cross between functional and bespoke;
- switching the focus of HR centres of expertise to employees as consumers;
- removing some of HR's compliance role so we can spend more time encouraging innovation and value;
- seeing contingent staff as a crucial ingredient for helping HR become more flexible and innovative; and
- creating an R&D function within our HR departments as a core function of what we do.

Trend 1: Moving from business partners to account managers

As an HR director, whenever I advertised for a new HR business partner I was tempted to change the job title to 'Superhero with Strong Interpersonal Skills'.

We need a strategic and commercial HR business partner. They must have experience in the full range of HR elements, be a coach, a law enforcer, a spoon-feeder, a tear-drier, and the conscience of the business. They must be prepared to come up with new ideas only to have them ignored, take the blame when things go wrong, and always have their item put last on any team meeting agenda – after finance, operations, marketing, IT, and problems with the toilets. They must be relentlessly cheerful and also prepared to listen to the ravings and woes of anyone who seeks them out. Above all, they must be able to present to their MD the latest group-wide HR initiative, which has no relevance to their own business unit, as the best thing since sliced bread.

When you look at what we want from HR business partners it's amazing we can find one, let alone in the quantity most HR structures depend on – especially when, in my experience, there are never enough HR advisers around with the capability to step into this role. Given this type of person is both scarce and expensive, we're seeing a shift in favour of an account management role. The account manager fulfils the business partner's strategic and commercial elements: the relationship-building, diagnosis of what's required, resource-planning, and oversight of the delivery. He or she then calls upon a pool of HR generalists and technical experts to deliver. This means we in HR gain a better strategic and commercial focus, as well as create a smaller pool of more flexible HR generalists who can go to the point of greatest need.

Trend 2: Moving HR advisory from transactional to helpful

All of us who bear the scars from outsourcing our well-loved and local HR advisers have learned some hard lessons. We've come to realize treating HR advisory as a purely transactional service we can economize on, by handing it over to an outsourced provider offering ruthlessly efficient processes, has major flaws.

What tends to happen in reality is because we've customized our HR processes over the years to be 'special and different' for us, it's impossible to streamline them when we transfer them; this creates extra costs as the providers navigate the various approaches we've accommodated over the years. Most critically, we forget the fact that when a line manager is asking about a particular policy she isn't actually asking about the policy but about *how to get around it*. The in-house HR adviser knew his line managers and employees and deployed a chunk of judgement along with his advice by weighing up the maturity of the manager, precedents that had been set, risks with a particular employee, and so on. This realization has led some organizations to bring this service back in-house.

Having said that, we're also seeing the emergence of next-generation providers who've built an understanding of the value and risks of HR advisory into their service. For instance, if a manager downloads a document with an element of risk attached to it such as a redundancy policy, this can trigger a proactive phone call to ask if the manager needs any help with its use. The way I see it, the HR advisory function will continue to be outsourced to a certain extent, but it will be combined with a human approach involving empathy, understanding, capability development, and the ability to assess risk.

Trend 3: Moving centres of expertise to centres of employee experience

As you know, treating employees as consumers is central to my approach, which means I'm delighted to see clusters of expertise focus more on the employee experience.

One of the (occasionally legitimate) accusations that's historically been levelled at these teams is they're too focused on producing the perfect recruitment, talent, development, diversity, performance management, or reward solutions instead of on connecting HR to the needs of the business. However, in the same way as consumer businesses often group their functions around a head of customer experience, so centres of expertise are starting to do this for their people by becoming centres of employee experience.

This is more than just a change of job title. By refocusing on what employees want at each stage of their life cycle, organizations can create a more joined-up employee experience that's greater than the sum of its HR parts. They can drive this through gaining genuine insights into their employees, create it by focusing on user-centred design, and deliver it in ways that are relevant to each segment of their employee 'market'.

Trend 4: Moving from compliance to capability

In my work as an HR consultant I'm often brought in to provide fresh challenges and ideas for HR teams. While they're excited by my suggestions they're often equally worried about being able to implement the changes, as their managers 'would never be able to do it'. They might be right, but this leads to a vicious cycle; we don't trust managers to manage, which means we produce rules and processes to make them do it, which means we spend our time enforcing and monitoring the process to make sure they have, which means we don't have time to develop their capability, which means we don't trust them to manage, and so on.

What's more, our reluctance to let go of the Employer Dad enforcement role seriously dents HR's image. If we spend most of our time keeping on top of operational compliance then why should we be taken seriously when we want to talk about creating value? This isn't an easy problem to solve – I've tried and failed often enough – but only when we release ourselves from the compliance burden and focus instead on building judgement, insight, and space for creativity will we be able to break the cycle.

The good news is this is starting to become a trend in HR, especially in organizations employing a high number of millennials. Interestingly, though, it's also gaining traction in sectors perceived to be less innovative, such as the public and not-for-profit. The continual cuts to support functions in these organizations have forced them to consider more radical alternatives than some of their less cash-strapped cousins. I know of many examples of highly productive results in the housing, education, and local government areas due to a rolling back of HR's role in compliance.

Trend 5: Moving from permanent to contingent HR staff

The accelerated pace of innovation in HR, the continued pressure on costs, and the need to solve problems as rapidly as possible should be leading us to question whether a standing army of HR people will be relevant in the future. It's true we've been using contractors, temps, and consultants to supplement or enhance our staffing levels for years, but they've usually been a tactical rather than a strategic choice. The growing trend is 'smart contingency', in which non-permanent staff are seen as a key part of any HR team. This gives us room to innovate and use our resources more efficiently, and is also an effective way to implement our projects. Rather than just bringing in additional people to fix a problem or cover maternity leave, or buying a consultant's time to give specialist advice, we can create a pool of talented people with a mix of capabilities to help us meet our medium and long-term needs.

Trend 6: Moving from business as usual to R&D

Rarely in HR do we think about innovation as a form of research and development. But if we want to provide a service to our people, much like a product department provides a service to its consumers, then we need to acknowledge the importance of staying ahead of the game.

The capabilities HR needs for the future

We've talked about the roles and structures we need in our teams, but what capabilities do we require? What do we in HR need to *be like* and *do well?*

I'll take it as a given that to be credible leaders at a senior level we need to be strategic, commercial, operationally savvy, and competent. But there are additional skills we must have, and activities we should embrace, if we're to improve performance and motivation in our modern, disrupted world. We must:

- get clever with how we use data to influence people;
- become the go-to experts on human beings;
- be willing to set the example; and
- get comfortable with giving away control.

Telling stories with data

To influence other people's behaviour we need a combination of facts and feeling. Marketing are brilliant at this – it's in their DNA. Whenever I ask HR professionals if they have a close working relationship with their marketing department none of them says yes, and as we saw in Chapter 4 ('Employees as consumers') this really shouldn't be an option any more. If we were to bring marketing capability into HR, we could tell far more effective stories with our data, about what our issues are today, and about how our companies could work in the future. Why don't you try swapping some of your HR blogs and magazines for marketing ones, and set aside time to build relationships with your marketing colleagues?

Another aspect of the combination of data with stories is technology and social media. We live in a world in which more than a billion job searches each month are on a mobile device, and yet a mere 26 of the Fortune 500 companies give their applicants the option of applying on a mobile. Just recently I did a survey of 20 high-up HR people in which I asked them whether they had their own HR social media strategy. None of them did. In fact most of them weren't even on Twitter because, like many senior managers, they're from a generation for whom it doesn't come naturally. We need to understand how social media can serve us, whether it be through apps that train and communicate, or through ways to close that gap between using technology at home and at work. If the people at the top don't see the need for the company intranet to be available on a smartphone, then how can they advocate innovation in other areas?

Becoming the human experts

When was the last time your finance director called you for advice on how to manage and motivate his people? Never? You'd not be alone. And yet his own team would be the first port of call for you if you wanted to know more about numbers. Recently I chatted to the head of HR for a major telecomms company who was feeling incredibly frustrated, even though he'd only been in the role for nine months (previously he'd been head of logistics for a major company). He'd been asked to write a paper on the company pay review, and in doing so had done a thorough market analysis and consulted with various people around the organization. On presenting it to the board he was shocked when everyone dived in with their own opinions and tore his proposal apart; in his previous role this would never have happened because they would have acknowledged him as the expert. In HR we're just not given the same respect.

Why is this? Partly it's because we're all human beings and therefore have our own views on what motivates us, which isn't unreasonable. But mainly it's because we've not done enough in this area to differentiate ourselves. We need to become the go-to people for insight into employees: who they are, how they think and feel, why they behave as they do, and how they relate to one another. It's not as if there isn't a treasure trove of books and articles out there to help us; authors Dr David Rock, Carol Dweck, and Dan Pink are great places to start. They've taken cutting-edge discoveries in neuroscience and applied them to the working environment; they're the 'human gurus' and we should be studying them.

Your goal is for anyone in your organization who's struggling to influence somebody, or motivate her team, to come to you for advice. And your take on their situation should be grounded in the latest research and most up-to-date thinking on human behaviour, rather than anecdotal or based on your own personal experience.

Setting a great example

In HR we must exemplify the mindset of disrupted world-ready leaders. We have to lead by example by becoming comfortable with ambiguity, being well connected and well read outside of HR, trusting people to perform well without having processes to follow, being happy with cross-departmental collaboration, embracing social media, being experimental with our teams, and, above all, being prepared to fail. If we can't embody the capabilities we want in others we won't deserve to be listened to with respect.

Ironically, the HR department is often the most hierarchical, process-driven, and least well equipped for the modern world of work out of any in the business. My business partner Karen, for instance, piloted an HR hot-desking initiative at the BBC; almost as soon as it was in place everyone put their own gonks and photos on their desks to mark their territory – it drove her crazy. Not being a great lover of hot-desking, I did sympathize with them, but nevertheless, if we can't put new behaviours into practice ourselves then what hope have we got of convincing anyone else?

We can change and we will – we just need to realize it starts with us.

Giving it all away

If we believe we're here to sit on top of people by creating rules and enforcing them, our minds will stay log-jammed with parental thinking. We have to be prepared to give away some control and become comfortable with doing so. Our new mindset needs to be one of enabling our employees to do the best work of their lives; it's not about us, our processes, or our status in the organization; it's about them.

When I read HR articles in the trade media they tend to focus on how we can get a seat on the board and build HR's reputation, and of course that's a good thing, but it's not the only way we'll make our companies fit for the future. To achieve this we have to remove the command-and-control behaviours we're also trying to reduce in our leaders, and which are holding us back. This isn't about giving away power, it's about gaining influence. So many of us steer away from this because we're afraid to lose what we've got; the role of policeman makes us feel important and valued, after all. But as long as we see our role as that of making employees do what they don't want to do rather than enabling them to become the people we need them to be, we'll be doomed to irrelevance.

It doesn't have to be this way. If we grasp the opportunity to change, we can create something so transformational and exciting that just imagining it takes my breath away. The only way our organizations will be able to cope and thrive in a disrupted world is if we redesign our relationships with our people. It's our competitive edge and true differentiator.

It's HR's time. It's your time. Let's do something different.

About the author

Lucy Adams is on a mission to change outdated people practices for good. Through her company Disruptive HR, she aims to provoke the HR community into creating new ways to support businesses in today's complex and ambiguous world.

Lucy has held board-level HR roles in a number of large organizations, most recently at the BBC. Lucy founded Disruptive HR having grown frustrated with the lack of innovation and fresh thinking in the profession. She and her team work with business leaders and HR professionals across the world to help them lead, engage, and develop their people differently. You can read the regular Disruptive HR blog on the website www.disruptivehr.com or you can join the Disruptive HR Club (www.disruptivehr.club) if you want even more content.

If you enjoyed this book and want to explore how to make change happen in a lot more detail, then check out Lucy's other best-seller, *The HR Change Toolkit.*

Notes

Chapter 1 HR is dead

[1] Barry, L. (2014) 'Performance management is broken', Deloitte, 5 March. http://dupress.com/articles/hc-trends-2014-performance-management.

Chapter 3 Employees as adults

[1] McCord, P. (2014) 'How Netflix reinvented HR', *Harvard Business Review*, January–February. https://hbr.org/2014/01/how-netflix-reinvented-hr.

Chapter 5 Employees as human beings

[1] Rock, D. (2009) *Your Brain at Work*. HarperCollins.

[2] The following excellent YouTube video summarizes this thinking. 'Drive: The surprising truth about what motivates us', Youtube, user 'RSA', uploaded 1 April 2010. https://youtu.be/u6XAPnuFjJc.

[3] Fernández-Aráoz, C. (2014) '21st-century talent spotting', *Harvard Business Review*, June. https://hbr.org/2014/06/21st-century-talent-spotting/ar/1.

Chapter 6 Recruitment

[1] 'United breaks guitars', Youtube, user 'sonsofmaxwell', uploaded 6 July 2009. https://youtu.be/5YGc4zOqozo.

[2] LinkedIn (n.d.) *The Ultimate List of Employer Brand Statistics for Hiring Managers, HR Professionals, and Recruiters.* PDF. https://business.linkedin.com/content/dam/business/talent-solutions/global/en_us/c/pdfs/ultimate-list-of-employer-brand-stats.pdf.

[3] 'Job interview at Heineken', Youtube, user 'yekowele', uploaded 20 February 2013. https://youtu.be/Aq6y3RO12UQ.

[4] 'The Snapchat pitch by DDB Oslo', Vimeo, user 'The Snapchat Pitch', uploaded 21 January 2014. https://vimeo.com/84663955.

[5] Covel, S. (2007) 'Start-up lures talent with creative pitch', *The Wall Street Journal*, 4 June. www.wsj.com/articles/SB118071923725321635.

[6] 'Next Jump culture deck', slideshare, user 'Next Jump', uploaded 5 March 2014. www.slideshare.net/NextJump/next-jump-culture-deck.

[7] Garcia, N. (2012) 'The emerging practice of strengths-based recruitment', HRzone, 13 January. www.hrzone.com/engage/customers/the-emerging-practice-of-strengths-based-recruitment.

Chapter 7 Induction

[1] Leung, I. (n.d.) 'How does employee onboarding impact new hire retention and turnover rates?', enboarder. https://enboarder.com/2018/11/01/employee-onboarding-new-hire-retention-turnover-rates/.

[2] *Business Management Daily* Editors (2013) 'Whole Foods employees vote on new team members', *Business Management Daily*, 19 March. www.businessmanagementdaily.com/34700/whole-foods-employees-vote-on-new-team-members#_.

[3] Bort, J. (2013) 'Awesome places to work: These startups have better perks than free food or beer on tap', *Business Insider Australia*, 22 May. www.businessinsider.com.au/10-awesome-ways-startups-have-hacked-their-company-culture-2013-5#commerce-sciences-has-the-last-person-to-join-create-a-welcome-kit-for-the-next-person-to-join-2.

[4] Burkhart, B. (2013) 'Getting employees off to a good start', *The New York Times* Blog, 13 March. http://boss.blogs.nytimes.com/2013/03/13/getting-employees-off-to-a-good-start/?_r=1.

[5] Bock, L. (2016) *Work Rules!: Insights from Inside Google That Will Transform How You Live and Lead.* John Murray.

Chapter 8 Employment rules and policies

[1] Valve (2012) *Handbook for New Employees.* Valve Press. PDF. www.valvesoftware.com/company/Valve_Handbook_LowRes.pdf.

[2] Prafull (n.d.) '5 Terrific examples of company social media policies', HireRabbit. http://blog.hirerabbit.com/5-terrific-examples-of-company-social-media-policies.

Chapter 9 Managing performance

[1] Buckingham, N. and Goodall, A. (2015) 'Reinventing performance management', *Harvard Business Review*, April. https://hbr.org/2015/04/reinventing-performance-management.

[2] Eichenwald, K. (2012) 'Microsoft's lost decade', *Vanity Fair*, 24 July. www.vanityfair.com/news/business/2012/08/microsoft-lost-mojo-steve-ballmer.

[3] Buckingham, M. (2015) 'Most HR data is bad data', *Harvard Business Review*, 9 February. https://hbr.org/2015/02/most-hr-data-is-bad-data.

[4] Estis, R. (2013) 'Blowing up the performance review: Interview with Adobe's Donna Morris', RyanEstis.com, 17 June. http://ryanestis.com/employee-engagement/adobe-interview/.

[5] Luijke, J. (2011) 'Atlassian's big experiment with performance reviews', Management Innovation Exchange, 16 January. www.managementexchange.com/story/atlassians-big-experiment-performance-reviews.

[6] Rock, D. and Jones, B. (2015) 'What really happens when companies nix performance ratings', *Harvard*

Business Review, 6 November. https://hbr.org/2015/11/
what-really-happens-when-companies-nix-performance-ratings.

Chapter 10 Reward

[1] Pink, D. (2011) *Drive: The Surprising Truth about What Motivates
Us*. Canongate Books.

[2] Heffernan, M. (2012) *Wilful Blindness: Why We Ignore the Obvious*.
Simon & Schuster.

[3] Koo, T.S. (2015) 'Why our startup replaced sales commissions
with monthly team bonuses', LinkedIn, 29 January. https://www.
linkedin.com/pulse/why-our-startup-replaced-sales-commissions-
monthly-team-tim-sae-koo/.

[4] PayScale (n.d.) 'CEO pay: How much do CEOs make compared
to their employees?', PayScale. www.payscale.com/data-packages/
ceo-income/full-list.

[5] 'Two monkeys were paid unequally: Excerpt from Frans de
Waal's TED Talk', YouTube, user 'TED Blog Video', uploaded 4
April 2013. https://youtu.be/meiU6TxysCg.

[6] DiSalvo, D. (2012) 'Study: Receiving a compliment has
same positive effect as receiving cash', *Forbes*, 9 November.
www.forbes.com/sites/daviddisalvo/2012/11/09/study-
receiving-a-compliment-has-same-positive-effect-as-receiving-
cash/#655e67926630.

[7] 'Tom Talks – catch someone doing something right',
YouTube, user 'NetApp', uploaded 11 July 2012. https://youtu.
be/O-JuGpwHQjY.

Chapter 11 Training and development

[1] Smith, D.A. (2015) 'What is Ebbinghaus' Forgetting Curve?',
LinkedIn, 20 August. www.linkedin.com/pulse/what-ebbinghaus-
forggeting-curve-darren-a-smith-das-/?trk=prof-post.

[2] Cisco (n.d.) 'Career development', Cisco. https://
learningspace.cisco.com/.

Chapter 12 Talent management

[1] Gratton, L. and Scott, A. (2016) *The 100-Year Life: Living and Working in an Age of Longevity*. Bloomsbury.

[2] Fox, K. and O'Connor, J. (2015) 'Five ways work will change in the future', *The Guardian*, 29 November. www.theguardian. com/society/2015/nov/29/five-ways-work-will-change-future-of-workplace-ai-cloud-retirement-remote.

[3] Kaplan, J. (2016) *Humans Need Not Apply: A Guide to Wealth and Work in the Age of Artificial Intelligence*. Yale University Press.

[4] Buckingham, M. (2015) 'Most HR data is bad data', *Harvard Business Review*, 9 February. https://hbr.org/2015/02/most-hr-data-is-bad-data.

[5] Hoffman, R. (2014) *The Alliance: Managing Talent in the Networked Age*. Harvard Business Review Press.

[6] Benko, C. and Weisberg, A. (2008) 'Mass career customization', Deloitte Insights, 1 August. http://dupress.com/articles/mass-career-customization-building-the-corporate-lattice-organization/.

[7] *Ibid.*

Chapter 13 Leadership development

[1] Babiak, P.B. and Hare, R.D. (2007) *Snakes in Suits: When Psychopaths Go To Work*. HarperBusiness.

[2] Egon Zehnder (2017) 'We know that leaders come in different packages and it takes patience to identify them', 1 January. www. egonzehnder.com/what-we-do/leadership-solutions/insights/we-know-that-leaders-come-in-different-packages-and-it-takes-patience-to-identify-them.

Chapter 14 Employee engagement and communications

[1] Goffee, R. and Jones, G. (2013) 'Creating the best workplace on earth', *Harvard Business Review*, May. https://hbr.org/2013/05/creating-the-best-workplace-on-earth.

[2] Engage for Success (n.d.) 'What is employee engagement?'. http://engageforsuccess.org/what-is-employee-engagement.

[3] Adkins, A. (2016) 'Employee engagement in US stagnant in 2015', Gallup, 13 January. www.gallup.com/poll/188144/employee-engagement-stagnant-2015.aspx.

[4] 'This is a generic brand video, by Dissolve', YouTube, user 'Dissolve', uploaded 21 March 2014. https://youtu.be/2YBtspm8j8M.

[5] Waber, B., Magnolfi, J. and Lindsay, G. (2014) 'Workspaces that move people', *Harvard Business Review*, October. https://hbr.org/2014/10/workspaces-that-move-people.

[6] Unilever (n.d.) 'Improving employee health and well-being'. www.unilever.com/sustainable-living/enhancing-livelihoods/fairness-in-the-workplace/improving-employee-health-and-well-being/.

Chapter 15 Turning old HR into new HR

[1] Sloan, N. and Parent, D. (2015) 'Performance management: The secret ingredient', Deloitte Insights, 27 February. http://dupress.deloitte.com/dup-us-en/focus/human-capital-trends/2015/performance-management-redesign-human-capital-trends-2015.htm.